Live or Let Die?

The Euthanasia Debate Revisited

by Dr David Holding

First published by
Words are Life, 2022
www.wordsarelife.co.uk

First published in Great Britain in 2022 by
Words are Life
10 Chester Place,
Adlington, Chorley, PR6 9RP
wordsarelife@mail.com
www.wordsarelife.co.uk

Electronic version and paperback versions available for purchase on Amazon.
Copyright (c) Dr David Holding and Words are Life.

First edition 2022.

The right of Dr David Holding to be identified as the author of this work has been asserted by him in accordance with the Copyright, Design and Patents Act 1988.

All rights reserved. Without limiting the rights under copyright reserved above, no part of this publication may be reproduced, stored or introduced into a retrieval system, or transmitted, in any form or by any means (electronic, mechanical, photocopying, recording or otherwise), without the prior written permission of both the copyright owner and the publisher of this book. No paragraph of this publication may be reproduced, copied or transmitted save with written permission or in accordance with the provisions of the Copyright Act 1956 (as amended).

Acknowledgements

I am most grateful for the encouragement and assistance I have received from many sources during my research for this work. In particular, special thanks must go to the staff of the Law Department at the University of Central Lancashire. I am grateful for their expertise in Medical Law and how they shared their opinions on the matters raised in this work. I also acknowledge the valuable input I have received from members of both the medical and legal professions. Thanks are also due to the numerous staff at the libraries and archives I have consulted. Their courtesy and assistance are always so generously given.

Finally, my sincere appreciation must go to my ever-supportive publisher, Lesley Atherton, for her total commitment to ensuring my work is of the highest standard. Her encouragement and enthusiasm know no bounds.

Dr David Holding 2022

About the Author

Dr David Holding studied history at Manchester University before entering the teaching profession in the 1970s. He taught in both state and independent sectors. During this time, he continued historical research culminating in both a Master's degree and a Doctorate. Having previously studied law, David gained a Master of Law degree in Medical Law, which enabled him to transfer to teaching legal courses at university. Since retiring, David has concentrated his research and writing on various aspects of local history, legal trials, forensic science and medico-legal topics.

Also by David Holding

Murder in the Heather: The Winter Hill Murder of 1838
This book is a unique account of a brutal murder that occurred on the summit of Winter Hill in Lancashire in 1838. The account draws on both contemporary media reports and court transcripts and examines the events leading to the killing of a 21-year-old packman. It details the trial proceedings of the only suspect in the case. The work concludes with a re-assessment of the case in the light of modern forensic investigation. The reader is invited to reach their own 'verdict' based on the evidence provided.

The Pendle Witch Trials of 1612
The book provides readers with a sequential overview of the famous chain of events that ultimately led to the execution of women accused of practising witchcraft in the county of Lancashire. It is presented as a chronological account of the famous trials at Lancaster Castle in 1612. This book introduces the evidence and interview transcripts that formed the major plank of the prosecution case and will appeal to both the general reader and local historian.

The Dark Figure: Crime in Victorian Bolton
This book provides an absorbing overview of crime in the Lancashire town of Bolton over the period 1850 to 1890. It is primarily based on documentary survey and analysis of court and police records covering the period. It assesses changes in crime over time and asks whether these relate to economic, social or political changes taking place at the same time. The reader is left to reflect on whether crime (in all its many forms) has changed over time.

Bleak Christmas: The Pretoria Colliery Disaster of 1910
This work charts the events of the Lancashire Pretoria Pit disaster in December 1910. It reflects on the devastation it left to many local communities whose main source of employment was coal. The main sources analysed are the Home Office Report on the disaster and the Report of the Inquest. The findings of these detailed legal reports are presented in a format that will supplement existing material on the event. The book will also provide a reference source for both local historians and the interested general reader.

Doctors in the Dock: The Trials of Doctors Harold Shipman, John Bodkin Adams and Buck Ruxton
This book takes the reader on a journey into the world of three medical doctors in England, each coming from a different social background but with one common thread going through their lives. They all stood trial for murder. In each case, the reader is presented with all relevant evidence available to jurors in the case. The overall aim of this work is to invite readers to exercise their judgment in reaching a verdict.

Forensic Science Basics: Every Contact Leaves a Trace
This work is an absorbing introductory study of the techniques familiar from numerous trials, media reports and TV crime dramas. It begins with the basic principles of forensic science then examines such aspects as the time of death, causes of death, weapons of crime, identification of offenders and much more. It provides essential reading for those who wish to gain a basic introduction to this fascinating area of science.

A Warning from History: The Influenza Pandemic of 1918
The 1918 Influenza Pandemic was one of the most deadly events in human history, and understanding the events and experience of 1918 is of great importance to pandemic preparation. This book aims to address questions concerning the pandemic's origin, features and causes to provide the reader with an appreciation of the 1918 pandemic and its implications for future pandemics. This work caters to both the science-orientated and general reader in this crucial area of global and public health.

The Lady Chatterley Trial Revisited
The 1960 obscenity trial of Lady Chatterley's Lover remains a symbol of freedom of expression. It is also a seminal case in British literary and social history and credited as the catalyst which encouraged frank discussion of sexual behaviour. This book introduces readers to the trial

itself, describing the prosecution and defence opening and closing speeches to the jury, and much more before culminating in the judge's summing-up and the final verdict. The reader is provided with all the evidence to reach a considered assessment of the case and a question to consider – can certain literature 'actually' corrupt, or does it simply encourage expensive court trials and boost sales?

The Oscar Wilde Trials Revisited
It is only given to very few people to be the principal figure in three Old Bailey trials, before three different judges, and at three consecutive court sessions, all in one year. This complexity is one of the fascinations of the 1895 Oscar Wilde trials. In addition, they embodied celebrity, sex, humorous dialogue, outstanding displays of advocacy, political intrigue woven with issues of art and morality. Wilde's prosecution of the Marquess of Queensberry from criminal libel, and Wilde's later prosecution for 'gross indecency', reveal a complex person at odds with a class-centred and morally ambiguous Victorian society. This work considers these famous trials in chronological sequence and invites the reader to participate as an observer and potential juror in the proceedings. Finally, the reader is encouraged to consider the evidence presented at each trial and arrive at their own conclusions. This work will be of particular interest to law students owing to the counsel's skilfully demonstrated advocacy skills. It also caters for the general reader with a particular interest in the presentation of criminal cases in the courts in England.

The Whitechapel Murders of 1888
The killing of five women in the Whitechapel area of East London in 1888 remains the greatest and most horrendous of all unsolved murder mysteries. It is the classic 'Cold Case'. This work takes a novel look into the case from the perspective of the criminal investigation itself. In this approach, the more speculative and conspiracy theories surrounding the 'Jack the Ripper' crimes have been avoided. The reader is offered insights into these murders by employing the modern forensic techniques of geographical and offender profiling, which shed new light on these serial killings.

Forensic Pathology Basics: The Dead Do Tell a Story
In this work, the reader is taken on a sequential journey of discovery into the fascinating world of Forensic Pathology, with no previous knowledge of the subject being required of readers. Beginning with the initial discovery of a body, the reader experiences the processes involving the forensic pathologist, from the initial examination and

identification of the deceased to the final autopsy. The reader will be introduced to practical applications of the pathologist's skills and techniques at each stage. Past criminal cases will be introduced to demonstrate the variety of scenarios in which the assistance of the forensic pathologist is vital. The overall aim of this work is to provide the reader with a fascinating insight into the largely unseen involvement of the forensic pathologist in death investigations. It is especially fascinating when the circumstances involve criminal activity. The manner and causes of death are discussed in detail and cover the main areas of injury. A glossary of medical terminology is provided to explain the various terms used in the text. The work concludes with a Selected Bibliography to enable the reader to pursue their research in those areas they find particularly interesting and relevant.

The Coronavirus Pandemic: An English Perspective
The Coronavirus (COVID-19) Pandemic of 2020 onwards has been described as the second most deadly event in recent human history. The first was attributed to the Influenza Pandemic of 1918. A comparison has been made between the two events because of the similarities between the two as regards high mortality, and because of the resultant impact the pandemics had on the social and economic structures of the countries involved. This work provides the reader with a comprehensive background to the origins of the virus, its subsequent rapid spread in England, and the government's responses and control policies implemented to halt its progress. This work will be of interest to both the science-orientated and the general reader, with a concern in this vital area of public health, and in the preparation for future pandemics.

Dr David Holding

Contents

Table of Contents

Acknowledgements 3
    About the Author 4
    Also by David Holding 4
Contents 9
Introduction 12
Definitions 16
    Voluntary Euthanasia 17
    Non-Voluntary Euthanasia 18
    Involuntary Euthanasia 18
    Active and Passive Euthanasia 19
    Actions and Omissions: Killing and Letting Die 20
    Intending Death and Foreseeing Death Will Occur 23
    The Principle of Double Effect 24
Euthanasia: The Law in the United Kingdom 26
    Change 'Unsafe' Law on Assisted Dying, Says Ex-Police Chief 31
Euthanasia in the Netherlands 37
    Article 40 39
    Article 293 39
    Article 294 39
    Case Study: The Office of Public Prosecutions v Chabot (1994) 42

Case Studies 49
The Anthony Bland Case 49
Legal Aspects of the Bland Case 51
R v Cox Case 58
Crown Prosecution Service: Policy For Prosecutors in Respect of Cases of Encouraging or Assisting Suicide 68
Introduction 68
The Investigation 69
The Decision-Making Process 70
The Evidential Stage 71
Encouraging or Assisting Suicide and Murder or Manslaughter 73
The Public Interest Stage 74
Public Interest Factors Tending in Favour of Prosecution 76
Public Interest Factors Tending Against Prosecution 79
Medical and Public Perceptions of Euthanasia 81
The BMA on Euthanasia: The Philosopher Versus the Doctor 81
Report of the House of Lords Select Committee on Medical Ethics (HL Paper 21, Session 1993-4) 87
Some Arguments For and Against Euthanasia 87
Autonomy and Individuality 87
Sanctity of Life 89
Public Opinion 90
Relationship between Doctor and Patient. 91
Advances in Medical Science 92
'Slippery Slopes' 92

    Other Arguments 94

    Imposed Safeguards 95

    Mercy Killing 96

    Penalty for Murder 98

    Voluntary Euthanasia 101

Physician's Views on Current Legislation Around Euthanasia and Assisted Suicide: Results of Surveys Commissioned by the Royal College of Physicians 107

    The Law in the UK 107

    Background 107

    2006 Survey 108

    2014 Survey 109

Biomedical Ethics and Euthanasia 112

    Conceptual Questions about the Nature of Ethical Killing and Letting Die 113

Selected Bibliography 123

Introduction

Euthanasia, which essentially relates to decisions concerning the end of life, has become a focus of public, academic and legal debate. These decisions encompass such moral issues as the 'sanctity of life', autonomy and consent to medical treatment. As such, euthanasia is a hotly debated issue in almost every country where reasonably well-settled constitutions are tested by medico-legal decision-making at the end of life. Even the medical profession can find no consistency in answering the important question of where the doctors' duties and the patients' rights lie. Not surprisingly, the medical profession includes both supporters of euthanasia and those opposed.

Advocacy of a duty to end a suffering patient's life as an act of medical-moral compassion will be met with an equally strong call for the medical profession to maintain the 'sanctity of life'. Strong calls will also be made to maintain the tenet of the Hippocratic Oath, which states:
"To please no one will I prescribe a deadly drug, nor give advice which may cause his death".

Case law, which emerged after the decision to remove ventilation and hydration to Anthony Bland (Airedale NHS Trust v Bland (1993) AC 789), has had to confront many aspects of end-of-life medical practice.

During this work, it will be revealed that there has been a widening of the circumstances where the courts have been willing to declare the non-treatment decision of doctors to be a 'lawful' act. In part, the medical profession recognises this expansion of circumstances that their work is sometimes as much about easing suffering at the end of life as saving lives.

The initial problem with the debate on euthanasia is one of definition. This difficulty arises from the different perspectives from which euthanasia may be defined. A supporter of the power of the individual to make decisions about when their death should occur would regard the term 'euthanasia' in a positive light. The term may also be seen by an 'enabler' to encompass both the 'active' or 'positive' ending of life. Similarly, the advocate of the 'right' to euthanasia may equally be considered an advocate of the 'right to euthanasia'.

The term 'euthanasia' has been generally regarded as the means of causing death by a 'positive act'. There are two definitions to be considered.

Firstly, a medical definition: "A quite painless death, the intentional putting to death by artificial means of persons with incurable or painful disease".

Secondly, a general definition: "The act of killing someone painlessly, especially to relieve the suffering from an incurable disease".

The common feature in both definitions is the notion of a 'painless end to a painful or incurable illness'.

There is also some common ground in that some form of activity is involved. This involvement of 'activity' or 'passivity' has become the main focal point for judicial intervention concerning the decisions at the end of life. However, one may not find a consensual or comprehensive definition of euthanasia. It may best be described as an 'umbrella term', which involves decisions about ending a patient's life. This focuses on the key issue of the legality or illegality of forms of euthanasia.

The factual issues that can impact the legal regulations of euthanasia are fairly wide but essentially centre on the difference between voluntary and involuntary forms of euthanasia. The resultant debate forms the subject of this work, which centres on whether there is a moral and/or legal difference between actively terminating life and creating those circumstances in which other causes of death will result, commonly termed passive euthanasia.

This work introduces the reader to such factors as the use of technology in medicine at the end of life, mercy-killing and assisted suicide, the importance of consent to medical treatment, active euthanasia as practised in the Netherlands and the legal position of euthanasia in the United Kingdom. The subject of euthanasia invites regular debate at both international and national levels because changes in medicine and the law affect us significantly.

It will become apparent that the key to an understanding and analysis of medical law is to consider whether the medical decisions still lie with the doctor or whether the patient has the right to control the decision-making process. Consent remains the crucial element in medical law in determining who can control when members of the medical profession intervene to save life or maintain health. English law is imprecise and uncertain, and doctors cannot always be given clear advice about the legality of various procedures they encounter. There is certainly some evidence that doctors do practise 'covert' euthanasia. If what is taking place in medical practice is acceptable to society, then it is argued that the law should be changed to set out clearly the parameters within which these activities occur.

If society disapproves of certain procedures, how then can they be controlled? On the one hand, some oppose legislation because the current uncertainty allows for maximum flexibility for a caring medical profession. Any proposal to clarify the current uncertainty polarises opinions sharply. Pro-life campaigners have sought unsuccessfully to encourage police and prosecutors to pursue any evidence of 'covert' euthanasia with vigour. Supporters of 'voluntary' euthanasia argue to the contrary with equal passion.

The uncertainties and doubts that affect public attitudes toward the euthanasia debate are compounded by a misunderstanding of the relevant law and its lack of clarity. This work aims to clarify these misunderstandings regarding the theory, practice and legal position of euthanasia to provide the reader with a clearer overview of this important aspect of medical practice.

Chapter One:
Definitions

'Euthanasia' is a compound of two Greek words, 'EU' and 'thanatos', meaning literally 'a good death'. According to Collins English Dictionary, the more generally accepted definition is 'The act of killing some painlessly, especially to relieve suffering from an incurable disease'.

Virtually every society subscribes to some principle that prohibits the taking of life. However, there are significant variations between cultural traditions regarding when the taking of life is considered wrong. Throughout the Greek and Roman periods, there was an acceptance of such practices as infanticide, suicide and euthanasia.

However, primarily Judaism and the rise of Christianity contributed to the general acceptance that human life has sanctity and should never be deliberately taken. This view of the absolute inviolability of human life remained virtually unchallenged until the sixteenth century when Sir Thomas More published his *Utopia*. In this work, he portrays euthanasia for the desperately ill as one of the important institutions of an imaginary 'ideal community'.

Later, British philosophers such as David Hume, Jeremy Bentham, and John Stuart Mill challenged the religious basis of morality, particularly the absolute prohibition of suicide, euthanasia, and infanticide. 'Mercy' for hopelessly ill and suffering patients and, in the case of 'voluntary' euthanasia, respect for autonomy have been the primary reasons given by those who argue for the moral permissibility of euthanasia. Today, there is widespread support for some forms of euthanasia, and many contemporary philosophers have argued that euthanasia is 'morally defensible'. For example, official religious opposition (from the Roman Catholic Church) remains unchanged.

Active euthanasia remains a crime in every nation other than the Netherlands.

Voluntary Euthanasia

When a person is dying from a progressive, debilitating disease, suffering considerable distress, and knowing that there is no prospect of recovery, that person asks their doctor to give them a lethal injection to terminate their life. After consultation with their family and health care team members, the doctor administers a lethal injection, and the person dies. This scenario is a clear example of voluntary euthanasia, defined as euthanasia carried out by the doctor at the patient's request, and for their own sake.

There is a close connection between voluntary euthanasia and assisted suicide, whereby one person will assist another in ending their life. Euthanasia can still be voluntary even if the person is no longer competent to assert their wish to die when their life is ended. One might wish to have their life ended should they ever find themselves in a situation where they suffer from a distressing and incurable condition, illness or accident. If this has robbed them of their rational faculties, they could no longer decide between life and death. If, while still competent, they had expressed their wish to die in such a situation, then the person who ends their life acts upon this request, thereby performing an act of voluntary euthanasia.

Non-Voluntary Euthanasia

Non-voluntary euthanasia is when the person whose life is ended cannot choose between life and death for themselves. Perhaps it is because illness or accident had rendered a formerly competent person permanently incompetent, without that person having previously indicated a wish for euthanasia under certain such conditions.

Involuntary Euthanasia

Euthanasia is 'involuntary' when performed on a person who would have been able to give or withhold consent to their death. Consent has not been given, either because they were not asked or were asked but withheld consent wishing to go on living. Such cases of involuntary euthanasia should, in reality, be very rare. However, it has been argued that some widely accepted medical practices (such as the administration of increasingly large doses of pain-killing drugs that will eventually cause the patient's death) or the unconsulted withholding of life-sustaining treatment do amount to involuntary euthanasia.

Active and Passive Euthanasia

We have defined 'euthanasia' as 'mercy killing', where A brings about the death of B for the sake of B. However, there are two different ways in which A can bring about the death of B. Firstly, A can kill B by administering a lethal injection, or secondly, A can allow B to die by withholding or withdrawing life-sustaining treatment.

Cases of the first way are typically referred to as 'active' or 'positive' euthanasia. Cases of the second way are referred to as 'passive' or 'negative' euthanasia. However, all three kinds of euthanasia (voluntary, non-voluntary and involuntary) can be either 'passive' or 'active'. There is widespread agreement that omissions as well as actions, can constitute euthanasia. However, philosophical disagreement arises over which actions and omissions actually constitute euthanasia.

It is sometimes denied that doctors practise non-voluntary euthanasia when they refrain from resuscitating a severely handicapped newborn infant. It may also be denied that a doctor engages in euthanasia when they administer increasingly large doses of pain-killing drugs, knowing that they will eventually result in the patient's death.

Others believe that whenever an agent deliberately and knowingly engages in an action or omission that results in a patient's foreseen death, it constitutes active or passive euthanasia.

Despite the great diversity of views, debates on euthanasia have focussed on certain themes. For example, does it make a moral difference whether death is 'actively' or 'passively' brought about rather than occurring because life-sustaining treatment is withheld or withdrawn? Must all available life-sustaining means always be used, or are there certain 'extraordinary' or 'disproportionate' means that need not be employed?

Actions and Omissions: Killing and Letting Die

At a basic level, to shoot someone constitutes an action. Failing to help a victim of a shooting is an omission. For example, if A shoots B, and B subsequently dies – this is an action. If C does nothing to save B's life and allows B to die – this is an omission.

The 'euthanasia debate' is essentially concerned with intentional actions and omissions. These are deaths deliberately and knowingly brought about in a situation where the agent could have done otherwise than what they did. In our scenario, that is where A could have refrained from killing B and where C could have saved B's life.

There are, however, some problems in distinguishing between killing and letting die – or between active and passive euthanasia. If the killing/letting die distinction rested on the difference between actions and omissions, then the agent who turns off a life-support system that sustains B is responsible for killing B. However, the agent who refrains from putting C onto a life-support system in the first place merely allows C to die. That killing and letting die should be distinguished like this has struck many observers as implausible. Inevitably, attempts have been made to distinguish them in some other way.

One plausible suggestion is that we understand killing as initiating a course of events that leads to death. Then we understand allowing to die as not intervening in such a course. According to this suggestion, administering a lethal injection would constitute a case of killing, whereas not putting a patient on a respirator, or taking them off, would constitute letting die.

In the first case, the patient dies because of events set in motion by the agent. In the second case, the patient dies because the agent does not intervene in the course of events. This raises the question, is killing a person always morally worse than letting a patient die? One of the most plausible reasons is that an agent who kills causes death, whereas an agent who allows a person to die enables nature to take its course. This distinction between 'making happen' and 'letting happen' is important because it sets limits on an agent's duties and responsibilities to save lives.

To kill someone or deliberately let someone die deprives that person of their life. Under normal circumstances, people value their lives, and to continue to live is in 'their best interest'.

This is particularly difficult where questions of euthanasia are an issue. In cases of euthanasia, death and not continued life is in the person's best interest. This then means that an agent who kills, or one who allows a person to die, is not harming but benefitting the person. Today, powerful medical technology allows doctors to sustain the lives of many patients who would have died only a few decades ago because the means were not available.

This raises the familiar question. Must doctors always do everything possible to save a patient's life? The majority of writers in both the ethical and medical fields agree that there are times when life-sustaining treatment should be withheld and a patient allowed to die. This view is even shared by those who regard euthanasia as the intentional termination of life that is always wrong. This raises the need for criteria to distinguish between 'permissible' and 'impermissible' omissions of life-sustaining means.

Traditionally, a distinction has been drawn between 'ordinary' and 'extraordinary' means of treatment. The distinction between life-sustaining means regarded as ordinary and obligatory, and those that are not, is often expressed in terms of 'proportionate' and 'disproportionate' means of treatment.

Consequently, a means is proportionate if it offers a reasonable hope of benefit to the patient. It is disproportionate if it does not. This distinction between proportionate and disproportionate means is morally significant. However, there is no distinction between the means of treatment. It is a distinction between the proportionate or disproportionate benefits different patients are likely to derive from a particular form of treatment.

The same treatment can be proportionate or disproportionate, depending on the individual patient's medical condition. It depends on the quality and quantity of life the patient is likely to gain from its use. For example, a painful and invasive surgical operation might be considered ordinary or proportionate if performed on an otherwise healthy 20-year old, who is likely to gain a lifetime.

Conversely, it might be viewed as 'disproportionate' if performed on an elderly patient suffering from some other serious disease. This understanding of ordinary and extraordinary means does suggest that an agent who refrains from using extraordinary means of treatment engages in passive euthanasia.

Intending Death and Foreseeing Death Will Occur

If A administers a lethal injection to B to end B's suffering, A has intentionally terminated B's life. This case would be uncontroversial.

However, has A also intentionally terminated the life of B when A seeks to alleviate B's pain by administering increasingly large doses of drugs that A knows will eventually bring about B's death?

In addition, has A terminated B's life intentionally when he turns off the respirator that sustains B's life, knowing that B will die as a result?

When administrating large and potentially lethal doses of pain-killing drugs, death is in no way intended or sought. Therefore, even if A foresees that B will die as a consequence of what he or she does, B's death is only foreseen and not directly intended. The direct intention is to kill the pain. This distinction between intended results and foreseen but not intended further consequences is formalised in the principle of double effect.

The Principle of Double Effect

The law condemns 'active' euthanasia on the ground of intent. The terminally ill are beyond curative therapy by definition, and their management becomes a matter of the relief of suffering. Achieving this may inevitably involve some risk to life, but it is the patient's comfort and not their premature death which is the intended outcome.

The terminally ill patient sets the scene for applying the concept of Double Effect. The principle here is that action with a 'good objective' may be performed even though the objective can only be achieved at the expense of the collateral harmful effect. However, the 'good effect' must not be produced through the ill-effect, and there must be a proportionate reason for allowing the expected ill to occur. It is implicit in this principle that the good effect must outweigh the bad, and this may involve a value judgment.

It might be ethically justified to administer pain-killing drugs in a dosage that simultaneously shortens the terminally ill patient's life. It would not be justifiable to give the same dose to a young man with identical pain who stood a reasonable chance of recovery. The seminal case in the UK is that of (R v Adams (1957), Crim Law Review 365).

Dr Adams was thought to have treated a patient who was incurably (but not terminally) ill with increasing doses of opiates. Following her death, he was tried for murder and acquitted. During his summing up, Devlin said:

"The doctor is entitled to relieve pain and suffering, even if the measures he takes may incidentally shorten life".

Devlin's classic direction was followed in another famous trial, that of (R v Cox (1992) 12. BMLR 38).

The law on euthanasia is now very clear. Acts committed with the principal intention of bringing an end to life are illegal, except where the patient performs them. Treatment may be withdrawn after a request from a competent adult, and this will not amount to homicide if death results. The legal prohibition of assisted suicide remains in place.

All of this involves a restriction on the individual's autonomy, which is unacceptable for some. However, legalising active euthanasia compromises the state's duty to protect its subjects and the integrity of the medical profession too deeply for general acceptance at present.

Chapter Two:

Euthanasia: The Law in the United Kingdom

The criminal law regards a potential offence of homicide as any wrongful act which results in the loss of life. Such an act may be intended to lead to the death of another, or it may result from negligence, recklessness, or a culpable omission.

The most serious homicide offence is murder, which carries a mandatory penalty of life imprisonment in Britain. When life is taken deliberately, the appropriate charge is one of murder. So if a doctor responds to a request from a patient to end their life and subsequently administers a lethal injection, that doctor will have acted with the necessary *mens rea* (intent) for murder. From a legal stance, it does not matter that the patient gave consent for the doctor's action; consent is no defence to a charge of murder. In addition, the doctor's motive that the action was, in effect, 'mercy killing' does not alter the fact that his action constituted murder.

The actual prosecution of doctors for euthanasia is relatively rare, although several cases can be highlighted. Two of the most prominent cases in England were Dr John Bodkin Adams in 1957 and Dr

Leonard Arthur in 1981 (R v Adams (1957) Crim Law Rev. 365 and R v Arthur (1981) 12 BMLR 1).

The issue was complicated in that one involved the administration of painkilling drugs for which there was medical justification and the other involved withholding treatment. The legal point was more focused on the more recent case of Dr Nigel Cox (R v Cox (1992) 12 BMLR 38). Dr Cox was convicted of the attempted murder of a patient he had injected with a lethal dose of potassium chloride.

In the absence of the technical reasons, which in this particular case, restricted the charge to one of 'attempted murder'.

Dr Cox could have been facing one of murder. The conviction of this particular doctor highlights the fact that juries are prepared to convict doctors who engage in consensual euthanasia. Dr Cox had treated his patient for a considerable period and was sensitive to her suffering. However, his mistake was to assume that acting in 'good faith' would be a defence from the full force of the criminal law. However, there are ways in which such actions can be mitigated even where the act contemplated is one of intentional killing when a relative caring for a patient in extreme distress takes the patient's life. In such a case, a successful plea of 'diminished responsibility' may reduce the charge of murder to the lesser charge of manslaughter (culpable homicide).

This could be applicable when there is medical evidence that the person responsible was suffering from some form of psychiatric illness when the act was committed. However, such a plea would not be available to a medical professional, a doctor or a nurse. The administration of fatal doses of drugs may not be necessary to achieve the goal of ending a patient's life. A decision to refrain from commencing a course of treatment, or the decision to withdraw a course of treatment already commenced, may have the effect of ending life. In reality, such decisions are made regularly. They are an inevitable part of the humane and conscientious practice of medicine. They are strongly defended by doctors and constitute an integral part of the medical treatment of dying patients. The criminal law does not require doctors to persist in treating a patient when no medical purpose is served in doing so. From a legal point of view, all that is required is that the patient is given such treatment as is medically appropriate in the specific circumstances. However, deciding what is 'medically appropriate' is of crucial importance.

For example, a decision to deny antibiotics to a young and otherwise healthy patient with a chest infection is significantly different from a decision not to treat a similar condition in an elderly patient with a poor quality of life and poor prognosis. So in the former case, the withholding of treatment could constitute criminal culpability. In the latter case, the law does accept that the limits of medical duty would have been reached. Consequently, there may be no further obligations to provide more than treatment which makes the patient comfortable. A difficult problem arises in the case of unconscious patients who are dependent on artificial feeding for their survival. Whilst there may be no duty to persist with medical treatment past the point at which such treatment serves any useful purpose, there is a clear continuing obligation to provide for the patient's basic needs. This has usually been taken to mean that the provision of food and water is legally required until such time when death intervenes.

In the case of a particular patient capable of swallowing, this requirement poses no difficulties. Such a patient must be given food and water even if medical interventions are abandoned. However, a patient in a 'persistent vegetative state' (PVS) may require nutrition and hydration by nasogastric tube. They may also be irretrievably unconscious and completely reliant on artificial methods to provide these necessities. Litigation in England has now clarified the position concerning such patients and related civil law cases.

In Airedale NHS Trust v Bland (see Chapter Four), the House of Lords considered the position of a young man who had suffered serious brain damage injury in a football stadium disaster and had entered into the persistent vegetative state of PVS. It was accepted by both the patient's doctors and family that there was no prospect of the recovery of consciousness.

In those circumstances, the hospital sought declarations to withdraw the nasogastric tube feeding the patient and allow him to die. The resulting judgments, both at the Court of Appeal and the House of Lords, displayed the sensitive treatment of an emotionally charged issue. These have met with broad general approval. At the heart of these appeals lay a view of the provision of artificial feeding as one aspect of medical treatment rather than a distinct medical duty. Once this was established, whether or not to continue with it could be resolved in exactly the same way as any other treatment decision. Consequently, the 'best interests' test could be invoked.

This raised the question; was it in the 'best interests' of Anthony Bland that his body be kept alive when his personality and humanity had been destroyed?. The court answered "No" to this question, and the patient was allowed to die.

The result of this case was that euthanasia had not been authorised. However, it did send a clear signal that human life need not be maintained at all costs when no possible conscious enjoyment or values could result from these efforts. Since the criminal law in England is so rigid in its condemnation of taking an active step to end life, can this legal 'obstacle' be avoided by providing medical assistance to enable patients to take their own lives?

The legal resolution to this depends on the nature of the assistance given and the circumstances of the particular case. In England, suicide was a crime until the passing of the Suicide Act in 1961. This legislation decriminalised suicide but retained the criminal prohibition of aiding and abetting suicide. This means that a doctor who responds to a patient's direct request to prescribe drugs that he knows the patient intends to use to take his life will be committing an offence under the Act.

However, successful prosecutions would depend on establishing a clear link between the provision of the advice and the act of suicide, which may be difficult to establish. The Crown Prosecution Service (CPS) in

England and Wales issued guidelines regarding encouraging and assisting suicide in 2010. In its introduction, the guidelines outlined the law concerning prosecutions being brought under Section 2 of the 1961 Act:

"A person commits an offence if he or she does an act capable of encouraging or assisting the suicide or attempted suicide of another person. The consent of the Director of Public Prosecutions (DPP) is required before an individual may be prosecuted. The offence of encouraging or assisting suicide carries a maximum penalty of 14 years imprisonment. Committing or attempting to commit suicide is not, however, of itself, a criminal offence."

Change 'Unsafe' Law on Assisted Dying, Says Ex-Police Chief

"The law on assisted dying is 'incoherent and unsafe' and must be changed, the former Metropolitan Commissioner Ian Blair warns today, ahead of a landmark report on helping the terminally ill to take their own lives. Lord Blair of Boughton, who spent four years as Britain's most senior police officer at the head of Scotland Yard, argues, "The law as it currently stands, is failing both those whom it seeks to protect and those tasked with enforcing it". Writing exclusively in The Independent on Sunday, Lord Blair argues the law "has not kept pace with modern life and modern science" and must be changed. He is a member of the Commission on Assisted Dying which will this week, recommend significant changes to the way the terminally ill are treated and the legal threat faced by those who help them die.

New figures released to Parliament last month reveal that police have referred 31 cases of suspected assisted suicide to prosecutors, but none has led to charges being brought since new guidelines were introduced by Keir Starmer, the Director of Public Prosecutions in February 2010. Lord Blair says the current arrangement means people must take a

"leap of faith"

that Mr Starmer

"will respond compassionately and not prosecute, trading off their respect for a loved one's dignity against the fear of prison".

He adds,

"At a time when they should be grieving, the current system forces relatives of loved one into a world of uncertainty that leaves the police and prosecutors torn between good practice and natural human sympathy".

Last month, a former TV producer Geraldine McClelland, 61, travelled to Dignitas to die leaving a letter that said,

"I don't believe that my brother and sister should have to break the law so that they can be with me when I die. Because of the cowardice of our politicians I can't die in the country I was born in, in my own home".

The Commission chaired by Tony Blair's first Justice Secretary, Lord Falconer, and set up by the think tank Demos, will publish its final report on Thursday. The 11-strong panel, including the Tory MP Penny Mordaunt, the Reverend Canon Dr James

Woodward and Dr Carole Dacombe from St Peter's Hospice, took evidence from legal, medical and religious experts. Witnesses included Alan Cutkelvin Rees, who helped his partner to travel to the Dignitas clinic in Switzerland to die in 2007, and Debbie Purdy, who has multiple sclerosis and has campaigned to know if her husband will be charged if he helps her travel to Dignitas said,

> "It's very hard to grieve for somebody when you've had your house turned over and you are on police bail for something".

Colin Broad, the former England Test cricketer, told how his wife Michelle, who had motor neurone disease, committed suicide alone.

> "Michelle had organised the end of her life remarkably well, left little gifts for her tennis club members and notes for me and the children. And the police just swooped up all those things and took them away."

Lord Blair says the report will make many recommendations and many caveats.

> "The creation of a humane, coherent and enforceable framework of law will be one of them".

Prosecutors say that in most cases suspects are "most reluctant" for the person to commit suicide but want to abide by the wishes of the individual. Mr Starmer insisted that current guidance "works well", though he declined to say whether he thought the law should be changed. He said the cases he has seen since the guidelines were issued are

> "broadly speaking, acts within a family, compassionate acts by individuals who very often lived with the deceased for a good period of time.

Very often in a relationship, often in a strong, loving relationship".

Investigating officers are encouraged to discuss cases with the Crown Prosecution Service early. All case files are referred to the Special Crime and Counter Terrorism Division in London, then to the DPP, which decides whether there is sufficient evidence to provide a realistic prospect of conviction, and that it is in the public interest to proceed. A financial investigation is carried out to see if money could have been a motivation for someone to help a loved one die. Police inquiries can take weeks or even months.

The new DPP guidelines were drawn up in February 2010, after Mrs Purdy's legal challenge reached the House of Lords. The CPS insists the policy
"does not change the law on assisted suicide, which remains a criminal offence".

A spokesman added,
"The guidelines are transparent and ensuring consistency in our approach, which has helped to build public confidence in the exercise and to ensure fair treatment of those most affected by the death of someone they love".

Lord Blair also raises concerns about the "lack of clarity" for doctors about what constitutes providing "assistance" to someone to take their own life. In the New Year, the General Medical Council is to draw up new guidelines on the punishment doctors should face if they are alleged to have assisted in a suicide, say, by giving information on suicide or providing practical help to someone to travel to Dignitas.

In the five years to March 2011, the Medical Protection Society received nearly 70 calls and 30 requests for written advice on the issue of assisted suicide from doctors and nurses, and

"while there is a relatively small number, it is a source of significant anxiety"

said Dr Stephanie Brown, MDS Head of Policy. Sarah Wooton, chief executive of Dignity in Dying, hopes the report will

"shed much needed light on the issue. The real debate should not focus on whether the law should be changed but on how it should be changed. We shouldn't be dismissing a change outright in the face of our clearly untenable situation".

Andrew Copson, chief executive of the British Humanist Association, said,

"reform of the law would be an important step to becoming a more compassionate and caring society".

Ludwig A. Minelli, founder of Dignitas, said in a letter to the Commission:

"At a time in which lonely, unassisted suicides among older people, in particular, are increasing sharply, as a result of the significant increase in life expectancy, and the associated health and social problems of many men and women who have become old, sick and lonely, careful and considered advice in matters concerning the voluntary ending of one's own life is gaining relevance. It is about time that the law makers in the UK (and other countries) respected the will of the people and implemented sensible solutions that allow individuals who choose so, to have a dignified, self-determined end to life at their own

home surrounded by those close to their hearts".

Most senior politicians have refused to support calls for a change in the law. In 2006, David Cameron wrote a letter to pro-life campaigners that stated:

"I do not think we should allow doctors and others positively to accelerate death, because I think the long-term consequences of permitting such actions are too likely to be dangerous for society".

A spokesman for the Ministry of Justice said:
"The Government believes that any change to the law in this emotive and contentious area is an issue of individual conscience and a matter for Parliament to decide rather than Government policy".

Source: The Independent on Sunday, 1 January 2012, pages 8-9.
Author: Matt Chorley.

Chapter Three:

Euthanasia in the Netherlands

Those opposed to the active termination of the 'competent' patient requesting death tend to point to the law and practice of euthanasia in the Netherlands. Their practice has significance for English medical law as it indicates a way forward to those in favour of physician-assisted suicide or PAS.

However, the legal situation in the Netherlands is complicated. It has been stated that voluntary euthanasia is tolerated by the prosecuting authorities. Providing that certain requirements are followed and procedural steps are taken, prosecutions will not generally follow, although voluntary euthanasia remains illegal.

However, this does not accurately reflect the legal position in the Netherlands. The Dutch Supreme Court has recognised that a doctor who carries out voluntary euthanasia in certain circumstances is not guilty of an offence under the Dutch Criminal Code. Consequently, he has the defence of necessity so that what he did was 'legal' and any subsequent prosecution would fail.

The important provisions of the Dutch Criminal Code are as follows:

Article 40

"A person who commits an offence, as a result of a force he could not be expected to resist, is not criminally liable."

Article 293

"A person who takes the life of another person, at that person's 'express and earnest request' is liable to a term of imprisonment of not more than twelve years, or a fine of the fifth category."

Article 294

"A person who intentionally incites another to commit suicide, assists in the suicide of another or procures for that other person the means to commit suicide, is liable to a term of imprisonment of not more than three years or to a fine of the fourth category, where the suicide ensues."

From these articles, it can be seen that euthanasia is explicitly prohibited by the two Articles of the Dutch Criminal Code. Article 293 prohibits 'killing a person at his or her particular request', and Article 294 prohibits assisting a suicide. Suicide itself (as in the UK) is not a crime in Dutch law.

In the UK, under section 2 of the Suicide Act 1961, a person commits an offence if he or she does an act capable of encouraging or assisting the suicide or attempted suicide of another person. The actual wording in the 1961 Act is 'aiding, abetting, counselling or procuring a suicide'.

In the UK, encouraging or assisting suicide carries a maximum penalty of 14 years imprisonment. In the Netherlands, the courts have held that Article 40 of the Criminal Code makes the defence of 'justification' available to a doctor charged under Articles 293 and 294. The first acquittal under this defence was in 1983 and was subsequently upheld by the Dutch Supreme Court in the Schoonheim case in 1984.

In this case, the Supreme Court held that a doctor could invoke this defence of 'justification' due to 'necessity'. The conflict between the doctor's duty to his patient whose suffering is 'unbearable and hopeless' and the requirements of the Criminal Code would be mediated through the care of the medical profession and the doctor's objectively justified decisions.

This legal opening created by the courts occurred during the 1980s and was subsequently reflected in Dutch prosecuting policy. Between the mid-1980s and the passing of legislation in 1993, there occurred an expansion and acceptance of the practice of euthanasia. This now offers the doctor a high degree of safety from prosecution if the doctor keeps within the accepted limits. In this sense, euthanasia in the Netherlands is no longer illegal. There also appears to be evidence that once the law opened the door to the practice of euthanasia, it could lead to a much wider practice being adopted.

As for the legal norms concerning euthanasia, legalisation is largely now complete. In the Netherlands, an informal agreement between the prosecution authorities and the medical profession has allowed the practice of active euthanasia for years. The prosecution authorities agreed not to prosecute any doctor who ended his patients' life within the parameters set by agreed guidelines. The patient must have 'freely requested' help in dying, and the physician must assure himself that the request is truly voluntary and well-considered. Both the patient and his or her doctor must be satisfied that there are no other means of relieving the patient's suffering. A second doctor must also be consulted. Until 2000, euthanasia remained formally unlawful in the Netherlands. Legislation to give legal effect to the earlier 'informal arrangements' was enacted in 2000.

The impact of the Dutch practice and their new laws has been the subject of much debate. What has been referred to as 'general' euthanasia does not apply to situations in which a doctor administers lethal drugs without the patient having made an 'explicit request'. So, death due to the administration of pain relief in doses known to be likely to shorten life is regarded legally and in medical ethics as subject to the doctrine of double effect. This is the case so long as the doctor's 'primary intent' is to relieve suffering.

Case Study: The Office of Public Prosecutions v Chabot (1994)

This case is an excellent example of the law and practice of euthanasia in the Netherlands. Ms B was 50 years of age, and for several years, she had undergone a series of traumatic experiences that had deprived her of all desire to continue living. Psychiatric treatment had little effect, and she had made one serious suicide attempt.

She was referred to a GP, Doctor Chabot, by the Association of Voluntary Euthanasia. After extensive discussions with her, Dr Chabot concluded that there was no question in her case of a psychiatric disorder or a major depressive episode. Her psychic traumas were, in principle, susceptible to psychiatric treatment, but Ms B consistently declined therapy. In Chabot's opinion, Ms B was experiencing intense, long-term psychic suffering, the suffering was unbearable and hopeless for her, and her request for assistance with suicide was well-considered.

Dr Chabot consulted a total of seven experts, and most of them agreed with his assessment of the situation and of the treatment perspectives. Dr Chabot has supplied lethal drugs to Ms B after she had requested them. He had been present when the patient administered them, and she died 30 minutes later. As required, Dr Chabot reported to the coroner that there had been a suicide in which he had assisted. As a result, Dr Chabot was charged under Article 294 and faced prosecution.

The District Court and the Court of Appeals found

the doctor's defence of 'necessity' well-founded. On appeal, the Supreme Court reaffirmed its earlier judgments that euthanasia and assistance with suicide can be justified if "the defendant acted in a situation of 'necessity' with a choice between mutually conflicting duties, he chose to perform the one of 'greater weight'. In particular, a doctor may be in a situation of necessity if he has to choose between the duty as a doctor to do everything possible to relieve the unbearable and hopeless suffering of a patient committed to his care".

The court rejected the prosecution's argument that this justification was not available in the case of assistance with suicide given to a patient whose suffering is non-somatic and who is not in the 'terminal phase'. It agreed that the wish to die of a person whose suffering was 'psychic' can be based on an autonomous judgement. However, the court did conclude that there was insufficient proof to support the defence of 'necessity' in the case. Since there was no statement available from an 'independent medical expert who has at least seen and examined the patient himself'.

Although the court observed failure to consult a colleague, whether or not the latter examines the patient does not, in an ordinary case, foreclose the defence of 'necessity', in the case of suffering that is not somatically based, evidence of consultation is essential. The judgment of the independent colleague should cover the seriousness of the suffering, the prospects for improvement, the alternatives to assistance with the suicide, and the question of whether the patient's request was voluntary and well-considered.

In this case, Chabot was found guilty of 'assistance with suicide'. However, no punishment was imposed upon him.

The fundamental basis for Dutch euthanasia law appears, with the decision in the Chabot case, to have taken a decisive step away from the doctor-centred approach, which has dominated legal developments toward patients' self-determination. Opponents of the decision in the Chabot case see it as an assertion of the 'Slippery Slope' toward 'involuntary' euthanasia. The Dutch system is not without its critics. It is argued that the system is 'out of control' in particular, that euthanasia is not always 'voluntary', that doctors fail to report deaths under the reporting requirements, and that euthanasia is resorted to at the expense of 'palliative care'.

However, such fears are simply not borne out by the facts. For example, there is a strong indication that psychiatrists in several jurisdictions, as a matter of professional fact, turn a blind eye to the fact that their patients are storing up medicines for a suicide attempt or do refer them to books on DIY suicide. Dutch law does not represent a departure from practice but recognises that it exists.

Euthanasia has been openly accepted in the Netherlands for a considerable time.
Whether there is abuse depends on the predilections of the reader and their interpretation of the statistical information. However, the scale of euthanasia's practice in the Netherlands (under both the earlier transitional provisions and now under the fully

legalised system) is a matter of dispute. Most studies, however, suggest that it is extensive. In 1991, it was estimated that nearly 2% of deaths in the Netherlands resulted from euthanasia, these involving approximately 2,300 cases of euthanasia and 400 assisted suicides each year.

This high incidence might give rise to concern. Still, the widespread disregard among doctors in the Netherlands for the formal requirements laid down in the transitional regime is even more disquieting. Such failures suggest that the practice's administrative or internal medical control is unlikely to prevent abuses. It would appear that euthanasia has been practised in many cases without the patient's consent. This could provide grounds for the suggestion that it becomes far more difficult to control the practice once an absolute prohibition against killing is removed.

Regarding the criticisms over the lack of control over euthanasia in the Netherlands, the following article provides a thought-provoking assessment of the Danish practice of euthanasia.

"The Netherlands are often criticised for their presumed lack of palliative care. The existence of only very few hospices in the Netherlands for example, is often interpreted as proof of a neglect of palliative care. Although much criticism is based on misunderstanding, the Netherlands does have some way to go in the provision of adequate palliative care. But what does this mean for a moral evaluation of euthanasia? By and large, there appear to be three ways of dealing with the issue of euthanasia. The first is to reject it on the grounds that it is forbidden by the principle of respect for life. Proponents of this view often also claim that euthanasia is not necessary at all. They believe that by paying sincere and close attention to the person who requests euthanasia, the 'question behind the question' will surely be revealed to be something other than a request for death, and that with good palliative care, extreme suffering need not remain unanswered. In this view, euthanasia and palliative care are incompatible.

An alternative response to the euthanasia issue stresses the importance of compassion. From this point of view, respect for life is of paramount importance as is good palliative care. Sometimes however, supporters of this view admit that sometimes illness and dying come with such suffering. If all other palliative measures fail, then euthanasia may be justified. The result of this view of euthanasia is the medicalisation of the end of life, since whether euthanasia is justifiable becomes largely a matter of medical discretion.

These two responses appear to differ primarily in their answer to the question: "Does intractable excruciating suffering exist?" However, even palliative care specialists will state that, unfortunately, it does. The real difference therefore, will be whether one allows the principle of respect for life to be overridden by other considerations in special circumstances.

Most proposals to regulate euthanasia follow the second view. This is also true of the official legal position in the Netherlands, where a conflict of the physician's duties is the basis for not prosecuting him or her, not the granting of a patient's right. There is no right to die in the Netherlands, nor is there an obligation for the physician to comply with the request of a competent patient to die even if certain conditions are met. From an official and legal point of view, therefore, euthanasia is only tolerated as a last resort. The reality of the Dutch euthanasia practices however, seems to be developing in another direction, with increasing emphasis on respect for patient autonomy. This could lead to a shift to a third approach, in which euthanasia is seen as a choice. Some patients do not want to live through suffering and decline even if pain can be controlled. They want autonomously to decide about how and when they die, and they want their relatives to remember them as they were when they were more or less healthy. They want to step out of life before the terminal phase really starts, and they want a doctor to do the lethal work.

This development is reflected in the data produced in all major studies in the Netherlands. The first nationwide study of end-of-life decisions showed that pain hardly ever was the sole reason for requesting euthanasia. In 1992, an independent study showed that in 56% of cases of euthanasia, requests were made because patients thought suffering to be pointless and in 16% because they feared the decline. The 1996 report showed that many patients asked for euthanasia to prevent more suffering. Further research in 1999, shows that the shift to autonomy is not a matter of patients only, but also of members of the public prosecution. The investigators showed that the presence or absence of an explicit request was the most important determination of the decision whether to hold an inquest. Life expectancy and type of suffering do play a role but a less important one.

This emerging sense that one does have a right to die means that more palliative care does not necessarily lead to a decreasing incidence of euthanasia. From a sociological point of view one may be tempted to interpret the shift towards autonomy-based requests for euthanasia as a by-product of a liberal society, with its emphasis on self-government, control and rational choice. To accept euthanasia in an individual case is one thing, to accept it on a public policy level is quite something else.

It is often argued that proposals to legalise euthanasia can never contain absolute safeguards. I think this is true; there is no rule that cannot (and will not) be broken. The question is whether this justifies a prohibition of euthanasia in an individual case. The Dutch tried to have it both ways by creating a public policy based on accepting and prohibiting at the same time. This created uncertainty and unclarity both for patients and physicians, and probably contributed to some critical reports being circulated.

Persuading the physician to bring euthanasia cases to the knowledge of the authorities is a problem for any euthanasia policy. The Dutch notification procedure helped to raise the notification rate to 41% in 1995. Since November 1998, five regional assessment committees have to advise the public prosecutor in all reports of cases of euthanasia."

Source: JM Van Delden, "Slippery Slopes in Flat Countries – A Response". (1999) 25, JME, 22. Quoted in Kennedy, I and Grubb, A, Medical Law, (Butterworth, London, 2000, pp 2007-2009).

Chapter Four

Case Studies

The Anthony Bland Case

On the 15th of April 1989, Liverpool Football Club were set to play Nottingham Forest in an FA Cup semi-final tie.

Six minutes after kick-off at Hillsborough Stadium in Sheffield, the game was abandoned following a crowd surge, which resulted in crush injuries to 766 Liverpool fans and 96 subsequent deaths.

One of those injured was 17½ year old Anthony David Bland. Emergency resuscitation from his injuries could not prevent Brain Anoxia, and this condition progressed to extreme Persistent Vegetative State, or PVS.

From the 12th of May 1989, Anthony was under the care of Dr James Howe, consultant physician at Airedale General Hospital, Keighley, West Yorkshire. In August 1989, Dr Howe expressed an intention to withdraw all treatment, including artificial nutrition and hydration. This was met with a warning from the Sheffield Coroner and the police that such action would constitute 'Murder'.

Both Mr Bland's parents and Dr Howe believed that such withdrawal of treatment was in Anthony's 'best interests'.

Supported by Airedale NHS trust as plaintiffs, they applied to the Family Division of the High Court for a declaration of lawfulness for the action they were proposing. The originating Summons to the High Court was issued on the 25th of September, 1992, which stated as follows:

"This Summons seeks declarations that the Trust and their responsible physicians may lawfully discontinue all life-saving treatment and mechanical support measures designed to keep Anthony Bland alive in his existing 'persistent vegetative state' including the termination of ventilation, nutrition and hydration by artificial means. That they may lawfully discontinue and thereafter need not furnish medical treatments to Anthony Bland except for the sole purpose of enabling him to end his life and die peacefully, with the greatest dignity, and the least pain, suffering and distress. That if death should occur following such discontinuance or termination, the cause of death should be attributed to the natural and other causes of the defendant's said persistent vegetative state. That such discontinuance or termination and any other things done or omitted to be done in good faith in accordance with the order should not give rise to, and should be without any crime or criminal liability on the part of the plaintiffs or any participant whether physician, hospital or others."

The High Court supported this primary application by its judgement of 19th November 1992. However, the Official Solicitor, who was appointed as *guardian ad litem* to represent Mr Bland as lacking the capacity for decision-making, appealed this judgment of the High Court. The Court of Appeal also upheld the decision of the High Court Family Division. The final appeal to the House of Lords was likewise unanimously dismissed by the five Law Lords appointed to review the case. In 1993, Anthony Bland's life-support measures were withdrawn, and he was allowed to die.

Legal Aspects of the Bland Case

In appealing the primary decision of the High Court, and arguments of the Official Solicitor were that firstly, withdrawal of artificial nutrition and hydration would constitute an act *intended to cause death* and, as such, it would be unlawful. Secondly, that discontinuation of artificial nutrition and hydration would constitute a breach of the doctors' duty of care for their patient.

Counsel for the Official Solicitor, Mr James Munby QC, argued that in allowing the withdrawal of basic life-sustaining treatment, the law would be, in effect, condoning 'euthanasia'. He also made a distinction regarding the duty of care, that artificial nutrition and hydration should be treated separately from other medical interventions.

The declaration allowing withdrawal was initially granted by Sir Stephen Brown, President of the Family Division of the High Court, in November 1992. It was subsequently affirmed by the judgment of the Court of Appeal on 9th December 1992. The Official Solicitor then appealed to the House of Lords, where the appeal was unanimously dismissed on 4th February 1993. The most important issue addressed by the House of Lords was that life-sustaining treatment may be lawfully withheld in an *adult patient lacking competence.*

Lord Goff of Chieveley noted:
"It would in my opinion, be a deplorable state of affairs if no authoritative guidance could be given to the medical profession in a case such as the present, so that a doctor would be compelled either to act contrary to the principles of medical ethics, established by his professional body, or to risk a prosecution for murder. *I do not consider that, in circumstances such as these, a doctor is required to initiate or to continue life-prolonging treatment or care in the 'best interests' of his patient".*

The judges addressed the Official Solicitor's Counsel's arguments in various ways. They emphasised non-malicious intent and consideration of the patient's best interests. If continuing to live could not be viewed as being in the 'best interests' of Anthony Bland, then treatment could be lawfully withheld, and to do otherwise, if done 'knowingly', would constitute both the acts of 'battery', and the tort of 'trespass of the person'. Removing or abstaining from a medical intervention judged not to be in the patient's best interest was to be viewed as an act consistent with a 'duty of care'.

It was also noted that from a purely philosophical point of view, given Anthony Bland's 'vegetative' condition, he may have had 'no interest' at all. An important distinction was made between 'allowing to die' through the act of omission and causing death through the act of commission. The latter is considered 'euthanasia' and therefore illegal.

The 'positive' act of commission, through which

death would occur, was the main argument of the Official Solicitor. Lord Browne-Wilkinson stressed:

"Apart from the act of removing the nasogastric tube, the mere failure to continue to do what you have previously done is not in any ordinary sense, to do anything positive, on the contrary, it is by definition an omission to do what you have previously done."

He added,

"The positive act of removing the nasogastric tube presents more difficulty. It is, undoubtedly, a positive act, similar to switching off a ventilator in the case of a patient whose life is being sustained by artificial ventilation. But in my judgment in neither case should the act be classified as 'positive' since to do so would be to introduce intolerably fine distinctions. If, instead of removing the nasogastric tube, it was left in place but no further nutrients were provided for the tube to convey to the patient's stomach, that would not be an act of commission. *Again, as has been pointed out, if the switching off of a ventilator were to be classified as a positive act, exactly the same result can be achieved by installing a time-clock which requires to be re-set every 12 hours, the failure to re-set the machine could not be classified as a 'positive act'. In my judgment, essentially what is being done is to* omit *to feed or ventilate, the removal of the nasogastric tube or the switching off of a ventilator, are merely incidents of that omission".*

It has been argued that the very concept of 'best interest' used to underpin the judgment in Bland is 'questionable'. Nevertheless, the principle of 'best interest' still holds for emergency situations, terminal cases or situations of perceived futility, often encountered in the intensive care environment. However, while artificial nutrition and hydration constitute 'medical treatment' and, as such, do not have to be given if deemed to serve no purpose, some may consider 'artificial nutrition and hydration' an appropriate 'comfort measure'. Wider implications other than the 'slippery slope' of the euthanasia debate were also raised in the Bland case.

Recent developments in medical science have fundamentally affected these previous certainties. In medicine, the cessation of breathing or heartbeat is no longer death, noted Lord Browne-Wilkinson. He, with others, considered it a matter of importance to bridge the gap between legal and moral duties in the context of evolving medical science.

When considering the importance of the Bland case to medical decision-making, it is important to outline the terminology encountered in this and other similar cases. The 'persistent vegetative state' or PVS is a neurological condition in which patients appear to be awake yet show no sign of awareness of themselves or of their environment.

In this condition, the concept of 'sleep-wake' cycles appears counter-intuitive but is attributable to the preservation of hypothalamic function. The vegetative state is considered part of a spectrum of disorders of consciousness that includes coma, minimally conscious state and 'locked-in' syndrome. Still, it excludes the 'locked-in' syndrome of conscious awareness with limited means of expression.

The 'vegetative state' is deemed permanent in the

UK if it is present for more than six months when the underlying pathology is non-traumatic or more than 12 months when the cause is traumatic injury.

Diagnostic difficulties are not uncommon, and while prognosis may be poor, the approach to long-term care varies on a case-by-case basis. The individual nature of each case underscores the need for referral to the Court of Protection should a decision to withdraw artificial nutrition and hydration in these circumstances be sought.

Many clinicians may feel ill at ease if asked to withdraw artificial nutrition and hydration in a stable PVS patient rather than when their condition is complicated by critical illness.

When considering advice from regulatory bodies, the General Medical Council (GMC) in the UK, states that

"all patients are entitled to food and drink of adequate quantity and quality".

It also notes that

"artificial nutrition and hydration (ANH) may provide symptom relief, or prolong or improve the quality of a patient's life".

From a pragmatic viewpoint, however, ANH is significantly removed from normal oral intake, with tubes, pumps, and formulated products bearing the hallmarks of medical intervention. It is also accepted that the benefits of feeding the dying patient are unclear. The consequences of interventions required to facilitate ANH and the process itself may add to the distress and overall suffering.

It should be noted that the GMC guidance has introduced a change in terminology from ANH to CANH (clinically assisted nutrition and hydration). The latter encompasses hydration and feeding via the IV route and through nasogastric and gastrostomy tubes.

However, the GMC still adopts the principle set out in Bland that CANH constitutes 'medical treatment' and, as such, should be treated as any other medical intervention that is subject to a 'burden of benefit' assessment. CANH may be withdrawn if deemed not in the patient's 'best interests' by all relevant parties. As a form of medical treatment, it should be noted that patients cannot demand CANH.

While the appeal of Anthony Bland's case was repeated unanimously, Lord Mustill's comments are still sound:

"It would in my opinion be too optimistic to suppose that this is the end of the matter, and that in the future the doctors (or perhaps the judges of the High Court) will be able without difficulty to solve all future cases by ascertaining the facts and applying to them the precepts established in the speeches delivered today. The dozens of cases in the American courts have shown that the subject is too difficult, and the situations too diverse, for the law to be settled by a single appeal".

While individual cases will continue to stir controversy, the judgment in the case of Anthony Bland and other similar cases have paved the road from case law to statute, contributing to the foundation of the Mental Capacity Act of 2005.

This Act makes provisions for persons lacking capacity by formalising assessment of competence for decision-making and determining best interests. The Act also allows forward planning for future loss of capacity with Advanced Directives and appointing individuals with Lasting Power of Attorney for personal welfare, including decision-making on life-sustaining medical treatment. However, it should be noted that such an individual would not be able to prescribe a course of action or omission that was not considered to be in the patient's broader best interests. The views of the next of kin as to the patient's values and beliefs are not invariably given an overriding weighting.

The unanimous decision of all eight judges involved in Anthony Bland's case reflected a need for a pragmatic approach to the evolving complexity of modern medicine. It was also a moral decision that required careful justification in legal terms, given the possibility of being viewed as endorsing euthanasia.

In defying death, modern medicine has forced a review of what constitutes an acceptable quality of life and the basis on which medical treatment should continue to be provided when meaningful neurological recovery is impossible. Against this backdrop, cultural/religious beliefs and legal restraints will likely continue to impact on withholding of artificial nutrition and hydration.

Given the emotive context, withdrawing nutrition and hydration will continue to be defined as a form of killing – and by the remainder of society as pragmatic but potentially inhumane. Knowledge of the legal, professional and public attitudes towards the withdrawal of ANH remains important for those making difficult end-of-life decisions.

Case References: Airedale NHS Trust v Bland (1993) AC 789. (1992) 12 BMLR, 64. 1 All ER (1992) 821.

R v Cox Case

Dr Nigel Cox was successfully prosecuted at Winchester Crown Court in 1992 for the attempted murder of his patient, Mrs Lillian Boyes. Mrs Boyes suffered from an incurable and increasingly distressing form of arthritis which made her hypersensitive to touch. This could not be eased by painkillers in its latter stages.

Dr Cox and Mrs Boyes had known each other for a considerable time and had talked frequently about these events. In fact, Mrs Boyes had extracted a promise from Dr Cox that he would not let her suffer. As the hypersensitivity to pain increased at the end of her life, Mrs Boyes and her sons repeatedly requested that the doctor end her life.

Dr Cox administered a lethal dose of potassium chloride, and Mrs Boyes died within minutes. Dr Cox was tried in an indictment alleging attempted murder because it could not be proved that the injection ended Mrs Boyes's life. Evidence was given during the trial that Mrs Boyes was only minutes away from death when the injection was administered. It appeared during the summing up that both the prosecution and the judge were aware of the near certainty that the potassium chloride was the cause of death. The trial Judge Ognall summed up the jury in the following terms:

"The prosecution allege that Dr Cox attempted to murder Lillian Boyes. They say that he deliberately injected her with potassium chloride, in quantity and in a manner which has no therapeutic purpose, and no capacity to afford her any relief from pain and suffering whilst alive. They submit that Dr Cox must have known that, and that in truth his conduct in giving that injection was prompted solely and certainly primarily by the purpose of bringing her life to an immediate end. Proof of murder, members of the jury, would require proof that the doctor's conduct actually caused her death. The prosecution have told you that having regard to Mrs Boye's condition on that morning, they cannot exclude the possibility though they would no doubt say it was remote, that, in fact, she died of natural causes between the actual injection of potassium chloride and her death. That is before the potassium chloride took its effect. It is for that reason, because they cannot exclude that possibility, however remote, that as you know, the charge you have to make up your minds about is not one of murder but of attempted murder, and I am sure you understand. If it is proved that Dr Cox injected Lillian Boyes with potassium chloride in circumstances which make you sure that by that act he intended to kill her, then he is guilty of the offence of attempted murder. You know, in this case, from the earliest stages that it has been admitted that he did indeed inject her intravenously with two ampoules of potassium chloride which no doubt you remember without looking at it ever again, his note at page 70 of the medical records clearly indicates.

According to her younger son Patrick, after

that injection, she just, and I quote: "faded away within minutes". According to Staff Nurse Creasey, she died, so she said, in a few minutes. Later she said about one minute after the injection. Thus, the giving of the potassium chloride in that form, intravenously, is admitted, I have said. The only question, therefore, for your consideration, ladies and gentlemen in arriving at your verdict, is this. Is it proved that in giving that injection Dr Cox intended thereby, to kill his patient? In the context of this particular case, what is meant, what do I mean as a 'matter of law' by 'proof of an intention to kill? We all appreciate, do we not, and certainly the evidence you have heard in this case demonstrates it, that some medical treatment, whether of a positive therapeutic character or solely of an analgesic kind, by which I mean designed solely to alleviate pain and suffering, carries with it a serious risk to the health or even the life of the patient. Doctors, as you know, are frequently confronted with, no doubt, distressing dilemmas. They have to make up their minds as to whether the risk even to the life of a patient, attendant upon their contemplated form of treatment, is such that the risk is or is not medically justified.

Of course, if a doctor genuinely believes that a certain course is beneficial to his patient, even though he recognises that course carries with it a risk of life, he is fully entitled, nonetheless, to pursue it. If sadly, and in those circumstances the patient dies, nobody could possibly suggest that in that situation, the doctor was guilty of murder or attempted murder. And the problem, you know, is obviously particularly acute in the case of those who are terminally ill and in considerable pain, if not agony. Such was the case of Lillian Boyes. It was plainly Dr Cox's duty to do all that was medically possible to alleviate her pain and suffering even if the course adopted carried with it an obvious risk that as a side-effect of that treatment, her death would be rendered likely or even certain. There can be no doubt that the use of drugs to reduce pain and suffering will often be fully justified notwithstanding that it will, in fact, hasten the moment of death.

And so, in deciding Dr Cox's intention, the distinction the law requires you to draw is this. Is it proved that in giving that injection in that form and in those amounts, Dr Cox's primary purpose was to bring the life of Lillian Boyes to and end? If it was, then he is guilty. If on the other hand it was or may have been his primary purpose in acting as he did, to alleviate her pain and suffering, then he is not guilty, and that is so even though he recognised that in fulfilling that primary purpose, he might or even would hasten the moment of her death. That is the crucial distinction in this case. It must confront you members of the jury, with a most exacting task in striving to reach, as I know you will, a true verdict according to the evidence.

I have told you that if Dr Cox's primary purpose was to hasten her death, then he is guilty. In using the words 'hasten her death' I do so quite deliberately, members of the jury. It matters not how much or by how little her death was hastened or intended to be hastened. I am sure you understand. You may recall Staff Nurse Creasey agreeing with (counsel for Dr Cox) that at the time Lillian Boyes received the first injection, not the potassium chloride but you remember the earlier one of diamorphine and diazepam, that at the time she received that first injection from Dr Cox that morning, she, Staff Nurse Creasey, considered that Lillian Boyes was only hours from death at best, and possibly only minutes away. Of course, there can be no certainty in that regard, but even if that be the case, no doctor can lawfully take any step deliberately designed to hasten that death by however short a period of time. Of course, members of the jury, to hasten the death, not merely alleviate suffering, it brings it to an end, does it not? A dead person suffers no more, but that is not what I meant by alleviation of suffering, nor am I confident what you understand me to mean by it.

Alleviation of suffering means the easing of it for so long as the patient survives, not the easing of it in the throes of and because of deliberate purposed killing. You will remember Professor Blake's evidence. A doctor's duty is to alleviate suffering for so long as the patient survives but, he said, he must never kill in order to achieve relief from suffering. To shorten life intentionally as one's prime purpose, he agreed, is unlawful, even though it may be the only means of alleviating the patient's suffering or pain. You must understand, members of the jury, that in this highly emotional situation, neither the express wishes of the patient nor of her loving and devoted family, can affect the position. You will understand and I tell you, that Lillian Boyes was fully entitled to decline any further active medical treatment and to specify that thereafter she should only receive painkillers. You remember she did that on 11th August. It is recorded in the notes and there is no doubt that was universally respected by the doctors and nursing staff thereafter. That was her, Lillian

Boye's, absolute right and doctors and nursing staff were obliged to respect her wishes. Dr Burne, a senior house officer, told you that he had told Lillian Boyes on that day when he had said, 'no more active intervention please, only painkillers from now on'...these are my words but I hope they reflect what he told you he said to her: 'this far and no further'. We will stop your positive medical treatment. We will confine ourselves to giving you only analgesics, only painkillers, but we cannot accede to your request that we give you something to kill you'.

How then, members of the jury, do you test what the Crown say were Doctor Cox's intentions, so as to answer that central question, namely was his primary purpose to bring her life to an end, or was it, or may it have been, on the other hand, directed primarily to alleviate her pain and suffering? The answer is that you do so by looking at all the circumstances of this case as you find them proved. You will look at Lillian Boyes's medical history, especially in those last days up to the day she died, 16th August, and of course, especially including that day. You will look at the expert evidence from the doctors and others experienced in drugs and toxicology, and you may think it of fundamental importance... to consider the nature of the substance finally injected by Dr Cox in those quantities into Lillian Boye's body. If you reach the certain conclusion that potassium chloride injected undiluted and intravenously as it was can only in Dr Cox's mind have been with the purpose of bringing her life to an end, then the charge is made out.

Dr Cox, as you know, is a highly-qualified, experienced and respected consultant physician.

What did he know of the properties and potential of potassium chloride used in this way? Let me identify for your assistance, members of the jury, what I understand to be common ground. First, that in the context of this case, potassium chloride has no curative properties. Second, that it is not an analgesic. It is not used by the medical profession to relieve pain. Neither this galaxy of talented medical men nor any written medical word has ever suggested otherwise. Third, that injected neat, as I shall put it, into a vein it is a lethal substance. One ampoule would certainly kill. According to Professor Blake, the injection here was therefore twice that necessary to cause certain death. Fourth, that any doctor would know that it would cause certain death and within a very or relatively short period of time. Fifth, that to inject two ampoules into Lillian Boyes intravenously, would cause her death within minutes, if not seconds. Sixth, that Dr Toseland gave the unchallenged evidence that there is no clinical use of which he was aware that could account for the use of potassium chloride in this way. Seventh, that Lillian Boyes was terminally ill. Once she had directed the doctors on the 11th August to abandon any treatment save for painkillers, it is beyond doubt that she had condemned herself to die, and within a relatively short time. To use the graphic phrase of (counsel for Dr Cox), she had signed her own death warrant. That brings me, members of the jury, to what I shall call a fundamentally important grey area so far as the defence are concerned, and it lies as I understand it, and I hope you agree with me, it lies in the suggested effect of the lethal dose of potassium chloride during the very short time between its administration and the consequential death.

Professor Blake agreed that the probable effect of the injection was to alleviate her suffering only by bringing her life to an end. But both he and Dr Dixon spoke of the relief of pain in the one, two or five minutes before she succumbed to the effect of that fatal injection. This is a crucial area so far as the defence is concerned. You may think, members of the jury, that you should approach that form of analysis with some care. First, because that is, or may be the effect for those few minutes does not of itself mean that this was Dr Cox's primary purpose. It is highly relevant but not definitive. You must be careful to distinguish effect on the one hand, and purpose on the other. Second, it is, I suppose, members of the jury, a truism that in many cases of death, there comes a time when the moribund person is on the very brink of death. It is a distressing subject but we have to look at it and it has been looked at closely in this case, has it not? There comes a time when the moribund, the inevitably dying person is on the very brink of death. You have heard as the jury in this trial evidence of the mechanics of death in this case. The heart begins to fail, the blood pressure is lowered, blood reaches the brain in progressively lower volumes, and as that occurs a deeper and deeper level of unconsciousness supervenes. Finally, the heart stops, the brain is completely drained of blood and therefore oxygen and breathing ceases, and at that moment the patient is dead.

In that sense, no doubt you will at once accept that the patient's pain and suffering are indeed progressively reduced, as the lethal dose takes effect, until the patient reaches the state described as dead. But, members of the jury, what you will have to ask yourselves, you may think, is this: is that as a matter of common sense and ordinary language saying any more than that even if, notice it, even if you purposely kill someone by drugging them you incidentally relieve their pain during their death-throes? So, you may have little hesitation, ladies and gentlemen, if any hesitation, in accepting that as the patient dies and because they are dying, their pain and suffering is during that time alleviated. Professor Blake and Dr Dixon told you so. The central question still remains, of course. Given that this injection of potassium chloride had the effect, not my emphasis, of alleviating her suffering, as she died, was that or may it have been Dr Cox's 'primary' purpose, or was it an incidental consequence of his proven primary purpose, namely to hasten her death? I come back to what Professor Blake said, I quote: 'It is probable that the effect of this injection was to alleviate suffering only by bringing her life to an end. By that means, Dr Cox, he agreed, keeping his promise to Lillian Boyes that he would ensure that she would die in comfort'. And of this aspect of the matter, Dr Dixon said: 'If no relief can be given other than by shortening life, and if the primary purpose of the doctor is to shorten life so that pain is alleviated, that is not proper'.

Dr Dixon agreed that having regard to this patient's unique grave condition he, Dr Dixon knew of no other way of controlling her pain, other than by bringing her life to an end. He said that he hoped that if confronted with that situation which, I understand he was saying mercifully he never has been, he told that if he were to be confronted with it, he would have had the courage to do what Dr

> *Cox did. Having regard to all those matters the defence submit that Dr Cox adopted which (counsel for Dr Cox) describes as an unorthodox way but nonetheless a way of relieving pain and suffering. It is submitted for your consideration that however rare, even unique, it may be to describe the administration of potassium chloride in this way in this case, it is fully justified and you cannot be sure that in all the circumstances, his primary purpose was to kill."*

The main issue for the jury was one of 'intent to kill'. The evidence indicated clearly that the injection of potassium chloride could have no 'pain relieving' effect, and the jury convicted. In sentencing Dr Cox to only one year imprisonment, suspended, the judge Ognall regarded the act of injecting as a breach of an 'unequivocal duty' toward a patient. The decision to prosecute in R v Cox has been criticised, as has the legal analysis.

While convicting Dr Cox, it still perpetrated the dual legal myth of 'double effect', introduced first in R v Adams 1957, concerning the doctor's action in ending the life of a terminally ill patient. Critics of the decision in R v Cox have pointed to the charge itself. There is a suspicion that the charge of attempted murder (with the flexible sentencing power of the court upon conviction) was manufactured. Rather this than the obvious full charge of murder because the latter carries an automatic life sentence upon conviction.

There appears to be a mixture of public policy in preventing the active termination of the life of the competent patient according to request (the conviction) and sympathy for the doctor's actions when the action is undertaken (the sentence). This case is a clear example of the legally indefensible medical law interpretation of 'double effect' and intention and the fiction of causation. The decisions allowed the doctor to escape criminal liability when using analgesic drugs in large doses, even when it was known that the dosage would accelerate death. The traditional legal notions of criminal law and causation have not been used in this case.

Crown Prosecution Service: Policy For Prosecutors in Respect of Cases of Encouraging or Assisting Suicide

Introduction

A person commits an offence under section 2 of the Suicide Act 1961 if they carry out an act capable of encouraging or assisting the suicide or attempted suicide of another person, and that act was intended to encourage or assist suicide/attempted suicide. This offence is referred to in this policy as "encouraging or assisting suicide".

The consent of the Director of Public Prosecutions (DPP) is required before an individual may be prosecuted. The offence of encouraging or assisting suicide carries a maximum penalty of 14 years imprisonment. This reflects the seriousness of the offence. Committing or attempting to commit suicide is not, however, itself a criminal offence.

This policy is issued due to the decision of the

Appellate Committee of the House of Lords in R (on the application of Purdy) v Director of Public Prosecutions reported at (2009) UKHL 45. It required the DPP

"to clarify what his position is as to the factors that he regards as relevant for and against prosecution"

(paragraph 55) in cases of encouraging or assisting suicide.

The case of Purdy did not change the law: only Parliament can change the law on encouraging or assisting suicide. This policy does not "decriminalise" the offence of encouraging or assisting suicide. Nothing in this policy can be taken to amount to an assurance that a person will be immune from prosecution if they carry out an act that encourages or assists the suicide or the attempted suicide of another person.

For the purposes of this policy, the term 'victim' is used to describe the person who commits or attempts to commit suicide. Not everyone may agree that this is an appropriate description, but in the context of criminal law, it is the most suitable term to use.

This policy applies when the act that constitutes the encouragement or assistance is committed in England and Wales; any suicide or attempted suicide resulting from that encouragement or assistance may take place anywhere in the world, including England and Wales.

The Investigation

The police are responsible for investigating all cases

of encouraging or assisting suicide. The Association of Chief Police Officers (ACPO) intends to provide all Police Forces with guidance on dealing with cases of encouraging or assisting suicide soon after the publication of this policy. Prosecutors involved in such cases should ensure that they familiarise themselves fully with the ACPO guidance when it is available.

The ACPO guidance will specifically recommend that police officers liaise with the reviewing prosecutor to seek his or her advice at an early stage and throughout their enquiries so that all appropriate lines of investigation, tin the context of the individual case, are discussed and agreed by the Prosecution Team. This is to ensure that all relevant evidence and information is obtained to allow a fully informed decision on prosecution to be taken. The reviewing prosecutor must ensure that he or she has sufficient evidence and information in order to reach a fully informed decision about the evidential and public interest stages of the Full Code Test. The reviewing prosecutor will need detailed information about the mental capacity of the person who committed or attempted to commit suicide and about any relevant public interest factor.

The Decision-Making Process

Prosecutors must apply the Full Code Test as set out in the Code for Crown prosecutors in cases of encouraging or assisting suicide. The Full Code Test has two stages: (i) the evidential stage; and (ii) the public interest stage.

The evidential stage must be considered before the

public interest stage. A case which does not pass the evidential stage must not proceed, no matter how serious or sensitive it may be. Where there is sufficient evidence to justify a prosecution, prosecutors must go on to consider whether a prosecution is required in the public interest. The DPP will only consent to a prosecution for an offence of encouraging or assisting suicide in a case where the Full Test Code is met.

The Evidential Stage

Section 2 of the Suicide Act 1961 was amended with effect from 1 February 2010. Therefore, prosecutors must identify the timing of any act of encouragement or assistance that it is alleged supports the bringing of a criminal charge relating to the suicide or attempted suicide of the victim. Where the act of encouragement or assistance occurred on or after 1 February 2010, section 2 of the Suicide Act 1961 as amended by section 59 and Schedule 12 of the Coroners and Justice Act applies. In these cases, for the evidential stage of the Full Code Test to be satisfied, the prosecution must prove that:

1. The suspect, did an act capable of encouraging or assisting the suicide or attempted suicide of another person; and
2. The suspect's act was intended to encourage or assist suicide or an attempt at suicide.

"Another person" referred to in Section 2 need not be a specific person, and the suspect does not have to know or even be able to identify that other person. The offence of encouraging or assisting suicide can be committed even where suicide or an attempt at suicide does not occur.

It is no longer possible to bring a charge under the Criminal Attempts Act 1981 in respect of a Section 2 Suicide Act offence by virtue of paragraph 58 of Schedule 21 of the Coroners and Justice Act 2009. Attempts to encourage or assist suicide are now captured by the language of Section 2, as amended.

Regarding websites which promote suicide, the suspect may commit the offence of encouraging or assisting suicide if they intend that one or more readers will commit or attempt to commit suicide. Section 59(4) of the Coroners and Justice Act 2009 adds section 2A to the Suicide Act 1961. Section 2A provides that a person who arranges for someone else to do an act capable of encouraging or assisting suicide or attempted suicide will also be liable alongside that second person for the encouragement or assistance. Section 2 A also states that a person may be defined as encouraging or assisting another person even where the suspect's actual acts can not provide encouragement or assistance. One example might be if the suspect believes they are supplying the victim with a lethal drug which proves harmless.

Finally, section 2 A also states that a suspect threatening or putting pressure on the victim comes within the scope of the offence under Section 2. The amendments to Section 2 of the Suicide Act 1961 are designed to update the section's language and make it clear that Section 2 applies to an act undertaken via a website in exactly the same way as any other act.

Prosecutors should consult the Ministry of Justice Circular 2010/03, which provides further detail about the changes made to section 2 of the Suicide Act. If the act in question occurred on or before 31 January 2010, then the former offence applies (aiding, abetting, counselling or procuring the suicide of another, or an attempt by another to commit suicide, contrary to the then section 2 of the Suicide Act). In these cases, for the evidential stage to be satisfied, the prosecution must prove that:

1. The victim committed or attempted to commit suicide; and

2. The suspect aided, abetted, counselled or procured the suicide or the attempt.

The prosecution also has to prove that the suspect intended to assist the victim in committing or attempting to commit suicide. It is also necessary to prove that the suspect knew that those acts could assist the victim in committing suicide.

Concerning an act done before 1 February 2010, it is possible in law to attempt to assist a suicide. Such an offence should be charged under the Criminal Attempts Act 1981. This enables a suspect's prosecution even where the victim does not go on to commit or attempt to commit suicide. Whether there is sufficient evidence of an attempt to assist suicide will depend on the factual circumstances of the case.

Encouraging or Assisting Suicide and Murder or Manslaughter

The act of suicide requires the victim to take their own life. It is murder or manslaughter for a person to do an act that ends the life of another, even if they do so because they are simply complying with the wishes of the other person concerned.

So, for example, if a victim attempts suicide but succeeds only in making themselves unconscious, another person would be committing murder or manslaughter if they carry out an act that causes the death. Even if they believe they are simply carrying out the victim's express wish.

A person who does not do anything other than provide information setting out or explaining the legal position regarding the offence of encouraging or assisting suicide under section 2 of the Suicide Act 1961 does not commit an offence under that section.

The Public Interest Stage

It has never been the rule that a prosecution will automatically follow where the evidential stage of the Full Code Test is satisfied. This was recognised by the House of Lords in the Purdy case, where Lord Hope stated that:

"It has long been recognised that a prosecution does not follow automatically whenever an offence is believed to have been committed".

He went on to endorse the approach adopted by Sir Hartley Shawcross, the Attorney General in 1951, when he stated in the House of Commons that:

"It has never been the rule that criminal offences must automatically be the subject of prosecution".

A prosecution will usually take place unless the prosecutor is sure that public interest factors tending against prosecution outweigh those tending in favour. Accordingly, where there is sufficient evidence to justify a prosecution, prosecutors must go on to consider whether a prosecution is required in the public interest. In cases of encouraging or assisting suicide, prosecutors must apply the public interest factors set out in the Code for Crown Prosecutors, and the factors set out in this policy in making their decisions.

Assessing the public interest is not simply adding up the number of factors on each side and seeing which side has the greater number. Each case must be considered on its own facts and on its merits. Prosecutors must decide the importance of each public interest factor in the circumstances of each case and go on to make an overall assessment.

One factor alone may outweigh several other factors, which tend in the opposite direction. Although there may be public interest factors tending against prosecution in a particular case, prosecutors should consider whether a prosecution should go ahead and for those factors to be put to the court for consideration when the sentence is passed.

The absence of a factor does not necessarily mean that it should be taken as a factor tending in the opposite direction. For example, just because the victim was not "under 18 years of age" does not transform the
"factor tending in favour of prosecution into a factor tending against prosecution".

It may sometimes be the case that the only source of information about the circumstances of the suicide and the state of the mind of the victim is the suspect. Prosecutors and investigators should make sure that they pursue all reasonable lines of further enquiry to obtain, wherever possible, independent verification of the suspect's account.

Once all reasonable enquiries are completed, the reviewing prosecutor should conclude that there is insufficient information if doubtful about the suspect's account of the suicide's circumstances or the victim's state of mind.

Public Interest Factors Tending in Favour of Prosecution

A prosecution is more likely to be required if

1. The victim was under 18 years of age.
2. The victim did not have the capacity (as defined by the Mental Capacity Act 2005) to reach an informed decision to commit suicide.
3. The victim had not reached a voluntary, clear, settled and informed decision to commit suicide.
4. The victim had not clearly and unequivocally communicated his or her decision to commit suicide to the suspect.
5. The victim did not seek the encouragement or assistance of the suspect personally or on his or her own initiative.
6. The suspect was not wholly motivated by compassion; for example, the suspect was motivated by the prospect that he or she or a person connected to him or her stood to gain in some way from the death of the victim.

7. The suspect pressured the victim to commit suicide.

8. The suspect did not take reasonable steps to ensure that any other person had not pressured the victim to commit suicide.

9. The suspect had a history of violence or abuse against the victim.

10. The victim was physically able to undertake the act that constituted the assistance to him or herself.

11. The suspect was unknown to the victim and encouraged or assisted the victim to commit or attempt to commit suicide by providing specific information via, for example, a website or publication.

12. The suspect gave encouragement or assistance to more than one victim who were not known to each other.

13. The suspect was paid by the victim or those close to the victim for his or her encouragement or assistance.

14. The suspect was acting in his or her capacity as a medical doctor, nurse, other healthcare professional, a professional carer (whether for payment or not), or as a person in authority, such as a prison officer, and the victim as in his or her care.

15. The suspect was aware that the victim intended to commit suicide in a public place where it was reasonable to think that members of the public

may be present.

16. The suspect was acting in his or her capacity as a person involved in the management or as an employee (whether for payment or not) of an organisation or group, a purpose of which is to provide a physical environment (whether for payment or not) in which to allow another to commit suicide.

The police and the reviewing prosecutor should adopt a common-sense approach regarding whether a person stood to gain. The suspect may gain financial or other benefits from the suicide of the victim after the suspect's encouragement or assistance.

The critical element is the motive behind the suspect's actions. If it is shown that compassion was the only driving force behind their actions, the fact that the suspect may have gained some benefit will not usually be treated as a factor tending in favour of prosecution. However, each case must be considered on its own merits and facts.

Public Interest Factors Tending Against Prosecution

A prosecution is less likely to be required if:

1) The victim had reached a voluntary, clear, settled and informed decision to commit suicide.

2) The suspect was wholly motivated by compassion.

3) The actions of the suspect, although sufficient to come within the definition of the offence, were of only minor encouragement or assistance.

4) The suspect had sought to dissuade the victim from taking the course of action which resulted in his or her death.

5) The actions of the suspect may be characterised as reluctant encouragement or assistance in the face of a determined on the part of the victim to commit suicide.

6) The suspect reported the victim's suicide to the police and fully assisted them in their enquiries into the circumstances of the suicide or the attempt and his or her part in providing encouragement or assistance.

These lists of public interest factors are not exhaustive, and each case must be considered on its own facts and merits. The evidence to support these factors must be sufficiently close in time to the encouragement or assistance to allow the prosecutor reasonably to infer that the factors remained operative at that time. This is particularly important at the start of the specific chain of events that immediately led to the suicide or the attempt.

Suppose the course of conduct goes beyond encouraging or assisting suicide, for example, because the suspect goes on to take or attempt to take the life of the victim. In that case, public interest factors may have to be evaluated differently regarding the overall criminal conduct.

Cases of encouraging or assisting suicide are dealt with in Special Crime Division at CPS Headquarters. The Head of that Division reports directly to the DPP. Any prosecutor outside Special Crime Division Headquarters who receives any enquiry or case involving an allegation of encouraging or assisting suicide should ensure that the Head of Special Crime Division is notified. This policy came into effect on 25 February 2010 and superseded the Interim Policy issued on 23 September 2009.

Source: Issued by The Director of Public Prosecutions – February 2010.
www.cps.gov.uk/publications/prosecutions/assistedsuicidepolicy

Chapter Five:
Medical and Public Perceptions of Euthanasia

The BMA on Euthanasia: The Philosopher Versus the Doctor

"The BMA report on euthanasia inevitably invites comparison with the excellent account and defence of current practice in the Netherlands by Professor Leenen. It comments on the licence given to euthanasia by social policy in the Netherlands, and presents a sharp contrast between practice and policy in the UK and in the Netherlands. The chief reasons why the BMA working party was able to reject the Dutch model of euthanasia centres on a question of fact and question of the purpose and function of law. The persistent argument of the BMA report is that in the kind of circumstances which Professor Leenen is presenting the doctor with, the moral necessity of killing in order to relieve suffering need not arise, and do not arise in this country. Techniques for the management of pain and terminal illness, as pioneered by the hospice movement, mean that few patients ever reach the stage where they have a persistent wish to be killed and the doctor feels that the only thing he can do for them is to accede to that request. The BMA report implies that it is because the development of palliative care is not so well advanced in the Netherlands, that the advocacy of euthanasia is taken so seriously in that country.

Professor Leenen's case for the legalisation of medical killing in appropriate circumstances depends in large measure on the argument that the function of law is to promote the autonomy of individuals, provided their exercise of that autonomy does not harm others. The BMA makes much of the fact that the function of statute and common law in this country cannot be seen in these terms. The facts that aiding and abetting a suicide is a statutory crime and that consent of the victim is not a defence against a charge of murder, indicate the weight behind this view. The question arises of whether an intervention designed to 'kill a patient' can ever be construed as anything other than one which brings harm to him. Where consent and autonomy are made much of in medical ethics, they are most plausible if seen as encapsulating factors which create a genuine partnership possible between doctor and patient. However, they cannot be regarded as licences to demand of the doctor procedures which bypass his/her own conscientious judgment as to what is harmful or not to human beings. They are conditions which prevent the doctor-patient relationship being manipulative of the patient, not ones which enable the relationship to become manipulative of the doctor.

The fact that common law and much reflective ethical opinion bids a doctor to respect a firm decision on behalf of the patient to refuse life-saving treatment and, in effect, choose death, cannot be used to overturn these points about consent and the limits of autonomy. The requirements in the common law tradition for licit medical treatment lay at least two duties on the doctor, the violation of either of which makes medical practice improper: not to treat without 'explicit' or tacit consent, and not to treat without a reasonable expectation of benefit. Forced treatment to save life against the patient's declared and certain wishes violates the first of these duties. If we regard killing as always a form of harm, as social policy appears to do at present, then effecting even voluntary euthanasia is contrary to the second of these duties. The opinion that killing patients is harming them and that there are no circumstances, short of treatment on the battlefield, in which doctors need to bring about death as the means of saving their patients from suffering and indignity, is only plausible to the extent that existing ways of managing the dying, the handicapped, new-born and the senile can be distinguished from seeking to kill in order to ward off evil.

WE all know, and the BMA report acknowledges the fact in some detail, that in many approved and accepted medical procedures, the hastening of death is the foreseen outcome of the doctors' acts or omissions. The main device which the BMA report uses to distance the acceptance of hastening death from the pursuit of death as a goal and benefit, in medicine, is the distinction between killing and letting die. Omitting to save or prolong life can often amount to killing. There is widespread agreement that it is possible through an act of omission to enact an intention to bring about death; therefore, it is possible to kill through omission. That decisions not to treat made by doctors can amount to killing patients... is one of the foreseen and intended results of the omission of life-saving treatment. If these assertions are correct, then any general use of the killing/letting die distinction will lead to confusion, since there are likely to be some killings through non-treatment and inaction, which hide under the label 'letting die'. There is considerable common sense behind the view that a doctor has killed his patient through omission, or at least hastened his death, if he has the opportunity to save or prolong that patient's life through some available treatment but deliberately withholds that treatment in the knowledge that death will occur or be hastened as a result of withholding it, and does so with the purpose that death should occur. So in many circumstances, to let someone die when the means and opportunity exist to save him is to kill him. In this respect, 'letting die' is a euphemism for 'killing'.

It would be extremely neat to be able to argue in all the cases styled 'letting die' that, through the bringing about of death was foreseen as a consequence of non-treatment, it was not actually intended. If this were the case, then the killing/letting die distinction would be a simple consequence of the distinction between death as one of the purposes of an agent's acts, and death as merely the expected side-effects of action. Medical killing through omission would not be killing if the principle of 'double effect' were then relied on to produce the conclusion that medical letting die occurred when the primary intent behind non-treatment was to avoid the infliction of a burdensome treatment, hastened death being merely a foreseen side-effect. It may be urged in defence of the special nature of medical 'letting die' that in many cases of death arising out of non-treatment, the patient's early death was inevitable and the omission of further life-measures was not an important cause of death, it merely hastened death.

Here lies a difficult point. It has been said that, since all must die, killing and hastening death are equivalent. Yet it is clear that we would not begin to think of non-treatment as a cause of death if treatment could only have prolonged life by an extra second. We have no criteria for deciding by exactly how much hastening death becomes causing death and killing. The BMA has argued that doctors remain legally and morally obligated not to kill and that in normal medical practice there are no circumstances where they need to plead to social morality or law to release them from this duty. In normal circumstances, their duty does not conflict with their duty not to kill. They have contended that the duty to care and comfort does sometimes absolve them of the duty to prolong life and therefore they are allowed to let patients die. It is the case that UK medical practice is shaped by the belief that in some instances, the duty not to kill clashes with the duty to care, and that sometimes the duty not to kill should give way before the duty to care.

One justification for killing severely handicapped infants might be found in the notion that, prior to the achievement of self-consciousness, no human infant is to be counted as a 'person'. They have not yet acquired the capacities that make something a person. Not being self-conscious creatures they are unable to value their own lives and their lives do not then deserve the unique protection we afford to lives of 'persons'. However, this principle that infants as such are not persons, and are not to enjoy the protection of our ethics and laws of homicide, is unlikely to commend itself. We know that the new born infant possesses potentially all the qualities that will make him or her worthy of the title 'human person', and for the respect for his or her life that goes with that.

We know that he or she is one and the same being as the later adult they will grow into. On these grounds alone, we will judge that, if they enjoy the protection of laws and principles forbidding homicide later in their life, they must enjoy them now. They cannot be viewed as a detached existent. When we turn to euthanasia and killing in medical practice, we can find evidence to support the judgment that contemporary law is in need of greater consistency in its treatment of medical and non-medical assistance to acts of suicide. Society cannot leave the determination of the scope and limits of the range of justified homicide in clinical practice, or of justified assistance in suicide, to doctors acting in isolation. These are matters for social policy, and the profession naturally has an important contribution to make."

Sources: British Medical Association: Euthanasia: Report on the Working Party to Review the BMA's Guidance on Euthanasia". (British Medical Association, London, 1988).'Medicine, Medical Ethics and the Value of Life', P. Byrne (ed), (John Wiley & Sons, Chichester, 1990), pages 15-33.

Report of the House of Lords Select Committee on Medical Ethics (HL Paper 21, Session 1993-4)

"In this report, the Committee sets out the arguments presented to it: (1) for and against Euthanasia; (2) for the introduction of a new offence of 'mercy killing' and (3) for abolishing the mandatory life penalty for murder.

Some Arguments For and Against Euthanasia

In this section we summarise the arguments which witnesses deployed specifically in support of, or in opposition to, decriminalisation of euthanasia.

Autonomy and Individuality

The chief argument of the VES (Voluntary Euthanasia Society) in favour of euthanasia
"is driven by modern concepts of personal autonomy, choice and the rights of the individual".

They pointed out that exceptions about the degree of control an individual may exercise over his or her own life have risen greatly, and that for many this extended to life's ending as well. Professor Dworkin also emphasised the role of autonomy and individual decision-making in matter of life and death. He said,
"I am in favour of choice because people disagree about what kind of a death is meaningful for them. I, myself, believe that what sort of death is right for a particular person and gives the best meaning to that person's life largely depends on how that life has been lived, and that the person who lived it is in the best position to make that decision".

He advocated euthanasia as an option for those people who felt that to be kept alive in a situation which they found unacceptable would be harmful to their lives as a whole, cheapening what they have valued. He said that many people would not wish to continue in a state of heavy sedation, if such were necessary for the control of pain, or in any form of permanent unconsciousness. He said,
"what counts as suffering is ending a life or allowing a life to linger, possibly for decades, in a form which the person whose life it is, and those closest to her or him, think is an insult or a travesty. This view was supported by some of the letters from the public which we received".

Professor Dworkin suggested that arguments against euthanasia on the ground that vulnerable people could be harmed by its practice, failed to recognise that other people could be harmed by a refusal to permit it.

The British Humanist Association suggested that
"to refuse a considered request is to treat that person with contempt".

The BMA on the other hand argued that, although denial of a right to euthanasia ran counter to the concept of autonomy and self-determination,
"granting the desires of some entails an unacceptable cost for others and therefore is contrary to other ethical imperatives such as the concept of justice".

The bishops said,
"A positive choice has to be made by society in favour of protecting the interests of its vulnerable members even if this means limiting the freedom of others to determine their end".

Other witnesses made the same point. The bishops also argued that the extension of autonomy to allow euthanasia would limit the autonomy of doctors, since
"patients cannot and should not be able to demand that doctors collaborate in bringing about their deaths".

Sanctity of Life

As we have seen, witnesses expressed a variety of views about the value of life. In addition, some witnesses argued strongly against euthanasia on specifically religious grounds. The bishops said,
"Because human life is a gift from God to be preserved and cherished, both churches are resolutely opposed to the legislation of euthanasia even though it may be put forward as a means of relieving suffering".

The Reformed Presbyterian Church of Ireland said,
"Life is to be viewed as God's gift, given and taken again according to his sovereign will. It is thus not at the disposal of any human being".

The Voluntary Euthanasia Society (VES) rejected the absolute concept of sanctity of life as one to which only a minority subscribe, and to which even the major religions see exceptions in certain categories of justified killing. They suggest that the phrase 'respect for life' may reflect the present day consensus on the matter more accurately than the absolutism of 'Sanctity of Life'.

The British Humanist Association suggested that sanctity of life was not a principle on which legal structures should be based, since it depended on a religious outlook which not everyone shared. They

suggested that,
> *"it is particularly hurtful to require someone who does not believe in God or afterlife, to suffer intolerable pain and indignity, in deference to a God or afterlife he does not accept".*

Public Opinion

The Voluntary Euthanasia Society cited both public and professional support for euthanasia in the form of opinion polls and press articles. They suggested that there is an informal human consensus on this matter is now beyond doubt and that legislation is necessary,
> *"to bring the law into line with current thinking on right and wrong".*

They said that the issue of euthanasia
> *"is now too much one of public concern to be left to the traditional discretion of the medical profession behind closed doors".*

Mr Ludovic Kennedy also suggested that public opinion was increasingly strong in support of euthanasia. Professor Jennett reminded us that both the Appleton Conference and a majority of the Institute of Medical Ethics Working Party had recently declared that euthanasia could be an ethically justifiable option in certain circumstances, and drew attention to other indications of a shift in some sectors of professional opinion.

Dr Tim Helme also drew attention to a number of surveys which suggested increasing support for euthanasia. He suggested there was a danger of the law falling into disrepute if it did not change to keep in line with public opinion. It must be noted however, that the results of the public opinion polls with the VES and Dr Helme cited, are far from decisive.

As with any poll, the result produced is much influenced by the way in which the question is worded. It may be doubted whether the expression 'to receive medical help to an immediate peaceful death' is readily understood to mean euthanasia. The omission of the word 'immediate' for the 1993 poll may be thought to cloud the matter further.

Relationship between Doctor and Patient.

The existence of a trusting and open relationship between doctor and patient is of particular importance when the patient is terminally ill and decisions must be made for care towards the end of life. The VES suggested that

"any change making it easier for doctors openly to carry out their patient's wishes can only reinforce confidence on both sides".

More witnesses however, felt that the relationship between doctor and patient would be undermined if the doctor was empowered to practise euthanasia, even under the strictest of controls.

The British Medical Association (BMA) said
"if doctors are authorised to kill or help kill, however carefully circumscribed the situation, they acquire an additional role, alien to the traditional one of 'healer' their relationship with all their patients is perceived as having and as a result, some may come to fear the doctor's visit".

The Linacre Centre suggested that the practice of euthanasia would corrupt the character of doctors, and encourage them to view some patients as lacking inherent worth.

> This would undermine
> *"a disposition indispensable to the practice of medicine; the willingness to give what is owing to patients, just in value of their possession of human dignity".*

Advances in Medical Science

The VES cited developing technology as a factor fuelling support for euthanasia.
> *"Having created the situation in which lives are routinely saved, transformed or prolonged by medical intervention, we can hardly pretend that the process of dying, and that alone, must be left to nature."*

Mr Ludovic Kennedy suggested that advances in medical techniques meant that
> *"the dominant fear today is of being denied release from a prolonged and undignified dying".*

This point was supported by a number of individual members of the public who wrote to us, particularly those who had witnessed the difficult death of a family member.

'Slippery Slopes'

The so-called "Slippery Slope" argument was clearly put by the BMA. They said that
> *"by removing legal barriers to the previously 'unthinkable' and permitting people to be killed, society would open up, new possibilities of action".*

They said that

> *"any moral stance founded on the permissibility of active termination of life in some circumstances may lead to a climate of opinion where euthanasia becomes not just permissible but desirable. Once actual termination of life is a matter of choice for competent people from such treatment becomes harder to defend".*

A number of other witnesses made a similar point. Sir Robert Kilpatrick observed that

> *"one of the great problems is always to work out the implications of a change because they may be much more reaching than one can see".*

He cited abortion as an example, saying that the number of abortions performed each year far exceeded that expected at the time legislation was passed.

Dr David Cook made a similar point:
> *"What began in 1968 as offering permission for doctors to perform abortions under certain restricted terms, has now become as expected, that abortion is available on demand, there has been a 'slippery slope' when legislation about justified killing has been introduced".*

The Reformed Presbyterian Church of Ireland feared that voluntary euthanasia would lead to a descent of the 'slippery slope' because of the need for concurrence by the doctor.

> *"The ultimate decisive factor is the patient's perceived quality of life, that his life is not worth living, not his request for death. There is no logical reason, once voluntary euthanasia is allowed, why the practice may not be extended to cases where no request has been made, if in the doctors judgment, that is the best course of action for all concerned."*

Other Arguments

The Royal College of Nursing (RCN) were concerned for the well-being of the vulnerable.

"We have daily contact with some of the most vulnerable people in society at the hardest times of their lives and we know that many of the problems that they suffer, they suffer as a result of poor resourcing. If euthanasia were an alternative then the imperative to provide the resources for those people, whether it is the education of doctors in pain control or provision of decent facilities for elderly people with physical illness, would be cut at a stroke."

A few witnesses considered that the knowledge that euthanasia was available as a last resort would comfort and reassure many patients who feared for the future, though in the event few might take that option. The Voluntary Euthanasia Society of Scotland (VESS) said,

"The ability to leave by the door marked Exit, should the final need arise, gives many patients the courage to go on much longer".

On the other hand, Mr Kennedy, although an advocate of euthanasia, acknowledged that

"some people are really terrified that if this becomes law they will be in jeopardy".

A number of witnesses emphasised that the time of dying would be a positive and productive phase of life, which could be sacrificed if euthanasia were an option. The BMA said that

"if handled well the crisis of impending death can be a time of personal growth and reconciliation for

all those close to the dying person".

Imposed Safeguards

Dr Helme set out a thorough and considered proposal for a framework in which, he suggested, euthanasia might be safely practised. He suggested that the law could allow a more limited right to be relieved of extraordinary suffering, a liberty to request euthanasia (rather than a right to demand it), reserved for exceptional circumstances. His proposal was for legislation to provide doctors who performed euthanasia with a 'special defence' to criminal charges if they acted in accordance with one of two procedures.

The first would involve notification in advance of the intention to perform euthanasia, and then retrospective scrutiny of the circumstances to ensure that the doctor had acted in accordance with prescribed conditions, if not, prosecution would follow.

The second procedure, appropriate in cases where the doctor was more uncertain of the circumstances, would involve application to a tribunal which would not have an automatic right to kill but could usually expect not to be prosecuted.

Dr Helme suggested that an advantage of his proposal was that, by making it clear that the practice of euthanasia was a statutory controlled procedure quite separate from ordinary medical practice, there could be no pressure to participate on doctors who objected on grounds of conscience.

The main safeguard proposed by the Voluntary Euthanasia Society was that euthanasia should be performed only if the patient had, at least 30 days earlier, signed a declaration requesting it, and currently repeated that wish.

They also suggested that where the request was prompted by treatable depression or anxiety, this should be observed and dealt with by the attending doctor. Professor Dworkin considered that it would not be possible always to be totally confident that a request for euthanasia was truly voluntary and not the result of pressure or coercion. But he suggested that a combination of legislative provision and social response could minimise the likelihood of such abuse. If euthanasia were permitted
"the message would be one of individual responsibility".

Mercy Killing

A number of witnesses considered the question, whether, in the absence of any change in the law regarding euthanasia, certain types of deliberate killing should be treated differently from others.

The Home Office discussed past proposals, that there should be a reduced degree of culpability for mercy killing. Their view was that to take motive into account would give rise to argument. They also suggested that the issue of mercy killing arose only infrequently, and that the courts often found diminished responsibility which enabled less stringent penalties to be imposed.

The Crown Prosecution Service (CPS) told us that it was not common for relatives or health-care staff to volunteer information in cases which might be regarded as mercy killing, so that there was often no police investigation. They also drew attention to other evidential difficulties in cases of that kind.

They reiterated that even in respect of a mercy killing by a relative, the CPS would feel obliged under the law as it stands now, the matter would be brought before the court as a case of murder.

Statistics which the Home Office supplied showed that between 1982 and 1991, mercy killing was an issue in 22 cases of homicide (in none of these cases was the defendant a doctor/relatives and other acquaintances of the patients were involved).

In all but one of those cases (where the charge was infanticide), proceedings were begun on a charge of murder, and a sentence of life imprisonment, the outcome. In the other cases where a conviction resulted, lesser offences were substituted and most of the sentences were for periods of probation or suspended imprisonment.

These statistics suggest two possible conclusions, on the one hand, it might appear that existing provisions are sufficiently flexible to allow appropriate outcomes to be achieved; on the other hand it might be suggested that the inadequacy of existing provisions is shown by the way in which the courts and prosecuting authorities apply them.

Mr Kennedy resisted the idea of a new offence of mercy killing, since it still implies an act against the will of the person whose life was ended, and so did not acknowledge the crucial voluntary element of euthanasia as he advocated it.

The Voluntary Euthanasia Society (VES) said that a new offence "would be better than nothing" failing the decriminalisation of euthanasia, but it would be unsatisfactory because it focused on the perpetrator rather than on the wish of the patient.

Sir Stephen Brown agreed to a suggestion that it would be useful if the law provided for different degrees of killing, one of them being 'mercy killing'.

Penalty for Murder

The fact that a conviction for murder carries a mandatory life sentence has been widely debated, not least by a Select Committee of the House *(Murder and Life Imprisonment Report of the Select Committee, Session 1988-89 HL. Paper 78-1).*

That Committee recommended abolition of the mandatory life sentence, which would allow judges to take account in sentencing, of the particular circumstances of each case.

Its report set out clearly the arguments for and against the retention of the mandatory life sentence. The most important objection was that, as the crime of murder is presently defined, the mandatory sentence applies to an enormous range of offences.

The Committee quoted Lord Hailsham of St. Marylebone's speech in *R v Howe,* in which he said,
"Murder, as every practitioner of the law knows, though often described as one of the utmost heinousness, is not necessarily so, but consists in a whole bundle of offences of vastly differing degrees of culpability, ranging from brutal, cynical and repeated offences to the almost venial if objectively

immoral, mercy killing of a beloved partner".

Among the factors which carried most weight with that committee in reaching its decision was the weight of judicial opinion in England and Wales. The then Lord Chief Justice, Lord Lane, and 12 out of the 19 High Court and Court of Appeal judges who expressed a view, were in favour of a discretionary sentence for murder, and the great majority of judges who took part in the vote in the House on the *Murder (Abolition of Death Penalty) Bill* in 1965, were in favour of a discretionary sentence.

Since the publication of the report on murder and life imprisonment, the House has had two opportunities to consider the law in this area.

The first was in the debates on the Criminal Justice Bill in 1991. An amendment to that Bill which provided that, in future, no court should be required to sentence a person convicted of murder to imprisonment for life was carried against the Government by a large majority.

Among the supporters of the Amendment were two former Lord Chancellors, the Lord Chief Justice, the Master of the Rolls and five Lords of Appeal. The Amendment was overturned by the House of Commons voting strictly on party lines.

The second attempt in recent years to abolish the mandatory life sentence was in a Private Member's Bill, introduced by Lord Ashley of Stoke. This was given a Second Reading on 8 February 1993, when the only speaker against the bill was the government spokesman.

With only a single dissent, the bill also completed its later stages and was sent to the Commons. In the debates on both of these bills, the main argument put forward by the government was that murder is a "uniquely heinous crime".

Most recently, an independent committee chaired by Lord Lane has repeated the call for abolition of the mandatory life sentence. That committee concluded that it was wrong to require judges to sentence all categories of murder in the same way, regardless of the particular circumstances of the case, and wrong to require the distinction between the various types of murder to be decided by the executive.

It suggested that one advantage of a change in the law would be to
"make it unnecessary for unsavoury devices to be adopted to evade the difficulties posed by the mandatory life sentence, the charge of manslaughter on the grounds of diminished responsibility being the prime example".

In evidence to us, the Home office repeated their view that
"the period of time spent in custody varies greatly from case to case, and that in practice the system is flexible enough to ensure that custody in not unjustifiably prolonged".

However, in 1990 and 1991, no prisoner convicted of murder served less that six years of a mandatory life sentence. The Voluntary Euthanasia Society (VES) reiterated the case for change. They said that the
"crudity of the mandatory sentence in no way reflects the enormous moral gulf which in reality separates the aggressive murder from the 'mercy

killing' carried out in response to a sufferer's own wish".

They also argued that
"the present rigidity of the law has led to hypocritical and degrading pleas which obscure the true facts of cases".

However, when asked to explain this, they gave few details. In its conclusions, the Select Committee rejected calls for changes in the law to allow voluntary euthanasia, and for a new crime of mercy killing.

Voluntary Euthanasia

The right to refuse medical treatment is far removed from the right to request assistance in dying. We spent a long time considering the very strongly held and sincerely expressed views of those witnesses who advocated voluntary euthanasia.

Many of us have had experience of relatives or friends whose dying days or weeks were less than peaceful or uplifting, or whose final stages of life were so disfigured that the loved one seemed already lost to us, or who were simply weary of life.

Our thinking must inevitably be coloured by such experience. The accounts we received from individual members of the public about such experiences were particularly moving, as were the letters from those who themselves longed for the release of an early death.

Our thinking must also be coloured by the wish of every individual for a peaceful and easy death, without prolonged suffering, and by a reluctance to contemplate the possibility of severe dementia or dependence.

We gave much thought to Professor Dworkin's opinion that, for those without religious belief, the individual is best able to decide what manner of death is fitting to the life which has been lived. Ultimately, however, we do not believe that these arguments are sufficient reason to weaken society's prohibition of intentional killing. That prohibition is the cornerstone of law, and of social relationships.

It protects each one of us impartially, embodying the belief that all are equal. We do not wish that protection to be diminished, and we therefore recommend that there should be no change in the law to permit euthanasia.

We acknowledge that there are individual cases in which euthanasia may be seen by some as appropriate. But individual cases cannot reasonably establish the foundation of a policy which would have such serious and widespread repercussions.

Moreover, dying is not only a personal or individual affair. The death of a person affects the lives of others, often in ways and to an extent which cannot be foreseen. We believe that the issue of euthanasia is one in which the interest of the individual cannot be separated from the interest of society as a whole. One reason for this conclusion is that we do not think it possible to set secure limits on voluntary euthanasia.

Issues of life and death do not lend themselves to clear definition, and without that it would not be possible to frame adequate safeguards against non-voluntary euthanasia if voluntary euthanasia were to be legalised. It would be next to impossible to ensure that all acts of euthanasia were truly voluntary, and that any liberalisation of the law were not abused.

Moreover, to create an exception to the general prohibition of intentional killing would inevitably open the way to its further erosion, whether by design, by inadvertence, or by the human tendency to test the limits of any regulation.

These dangers are such that we believe that any decriminalisation of voluntary euthanasia would give rise to more grave problems than those it sought to address.

Fear of what some witnesses referred to as a 'slippery slope' could itself be damaging. We are also concerned that vulnerable people, the elderly, lonely, sick and or distressed, would feel pressure, whether real or imagined, to request early death. We accept that, for the most part, requests resulting from such pressure or from remediable depressive illness would be identified as such by doctors and managed appropriately.

Nevertheless, we believe that the message which society sends to vulnerable and disadvantaged people should not however, obliquely, encourage them to seek death, but should assure them of our care and support in life. Some of those who advocated voluntary euthanasia did so because they feared their lives were being prolonged by aggressive medical treatment beyond the point at which the individual felt that continued life was no longer a benefit but a burden.

But in the light of the consensus which is steadily

emerging, over the circumstances in which life-prolonging treatment may be withdrawn or not initiated, we consider that such fears may increasingly be allayed.

We welcome moves by the medical professional bodies to ensure more senior oversight of practice in casualty departments, as a step towards discouraging inappropriate aggressive treatment by less experienced practitioners.

Furthermore, there is good evidence that, through the outstanding achievement of those who work in the field of palliative care, the pain and distress of terminal illness can be adequately relieved in the vast majority of cases.

Such care is available not only within hospices, thanks to the increasing dissemination of best practice by means of home-care teams and training for general practitioners, palliative care is becoming more widely available in the health service, in hospitals and in the community, although much remains to be done. With the necessary political will, such care could be made available to all who could benefit from it.

We strongly commend the development and growth of palliative care services. We have considered suggestions that, although deliberate killing should remain a criminal offence, killing to relieve suffering (that is deliberate killing with a merciful motive) should not be murder, but a new offence of 'mercy killing' should be created.

At present, the offence of murder embraces acts of deliberate killing which vary enormously in their character and which most people would agree vary "in degree of moral guilt".

The significant question however is whether the law could or should make distinctions between them. We consider that it should not. To distinguish between murder and 'mercy killing' would be to cross the line which prohibits any intentional killing, a line which we think is essential to preserve. No do we believe that 'mercy killing' could be adequately defined, since it would involve determining precisely what constituted motive. For those reasons we do not recommend the creation of a new offence.

Penalty for Murder

Pressure for a new offence of 'mercy-killing' arises mainly because of the perceived injustice of the mandatory life sentence for murder. We strongly endorse the recommendation of a previous Select Committee *(Murder and Life Imprisonment Report of the Select Committee Sessions 1988-89 HL Paper 78-1)* that the mandatory life sentence should be abolished.

This would enable the judicial process to take proper account of the circumstances of a case and the motives of the accused. It would avoid the law being brought into disrepute either by the mandatory imposition of a life sentence in respect of an act which was widely thought to be compassionate and (by some) arguably justifiable, or by the inappropriate substitution of lesser charges where it was expected that a jury would not convict for murder because of the mandatory life sentence. It would also give scope for an effective life sentence to be imposed where the circumstances made it appropriate."

In its response, the Government agreed with the Select Committee's view and turned its face against any reform. As regards euthanasia, the Government stated it was its firm view that the deliberate taking of life should remain illegal. As regards the introduction of a new offence of 'mercy-killing', the Government said to do so would undermine the law's uncompromising attitude towards deliberate killing and might bring with it, many of the dangers associated with the legislation of euthanasia. As for the mandatory life sentence for murder, that should stay to mark the unique nature of the offence of murder."

Source: Kennedy and Grubb: Medical Law, 3rd Edition (Butterworths, London, 2000, Pages 1966-1972).

Dr David Holding

Physician's Views on Current Legislation Around Euthanasia and Assisted Suicide: Results of Surveys Commissioned by the Royal College of Physicians

"Euthanasia and physician-assisted suicide have always been the subject of intense debate across society. In 2006 and in 2014, the Royal College of Physicians surveyed its members for their opinions on the subject. The results of these surveys are summarised here.

The Law in the UK

It is illegal, under Section 2 (1) of the 1961 Suicide Act to encourage or assist the suicide of another person in England and Wales – "Aid, Abet, Counsel or Procure". This was amended by the Coroners and Justice Act, 2009, which states that any person who 'encourages or assists another to commit suicide, shall be liable on conviction to imprisonment for a term not exceeding fourteen years'. Attempting to kill yourself (attempted suicide) is not a criminal act. Euthanasia is regarded as either manslaughter or murder, depending on circumstances. It is punishable by up to life imprisonment. There is no specific law on assisted suicide in Scotland, but anyone assisting the suicide of another person would be prosecuted for murder.

Background

Physician-assisted dying (PA) is the overarching term encompassing both euthanasia and physician-assisted suicide, or PAS, which describes physician involvement in the 'intentional' termination of a patient's life. The fundamental difference between euthanasia and PAS is the 'degree of physician involvement'. The Royal College of Physicians (RCP) carried out two surveys to gauge the views of its members and fellows on physician-assisted dying. The first was in 2006, the second in 2014.

2006 Survey

The survey asked respondents to consider the following key statement:

"We believe that with improvements in palliative care, good clinical care can be provided within existing legislation, and that patients can die with dignity. A change in legislation is not needed. Do you agree?"

The large majority of respondents, 3,741 people (73.2%) answered that a change in legislation was not needed, leaving a minority of 26% supporting a change in the law. The survey went on to ask members to consider the next key statement:

"Regardless of your support or opposition to change, in the event of legislation receiving royal assent, would you personally be prepared to participate actively in a process to enable a patient to terminate his or her own life?"

In contrast to the first question, only 59.4% answered NO, while 18.9% said they would actively participate in PAS, leaving 19.4% uncertain. As a result of the 2006 Survey, the RCP indicated its opposition to the Bill and did not advocate for a change in the law. Instead, the RCP called for a campaign for better End of Life Care (E ol.C) within existing legislation.

2014 Survey

The Survey was sent to 21,674 members with 8,767 responding (40%). As in the 2006 Survey, members were asked to respond to the first key statement. The majority of respondents, 4,179 people (62.5%) answered that a change in legislation was not needed, leaving a minority of 2,507 (37.5%) supporting a change in the law. The first question was asked:
> *"Do you support a change in the law to permit assisted suicide by the terminally ill, with the assistance of doctors?"*

The majority of respondents, 3858 people (58%) said NO, compared with 2,168 people (32%) who said YES. A further 10% answered YES, but not by doctors. Unlike the original Survey, the 2014 Survey asked members how they felt the RCP should position itself in the debate:
> *"What should the College's position be on 'assisted dying' as defined in the RCP's consultation document?"*

Of members answering the question, 6,697 respondents (44.4%) felt the RCP should be opposed to a change in legislation, compared with 24.6% in favour of supporting change, while 31% felt the RCP should remain neutral, or take no stance. Similar to the 2006 Survey, members were asked the same question:
> *"Would you personally be prepared to participate actively in assisted dying?*

There was a similar response to the 2006 Survey; 58.4% were opposed, 21.4% in favour and 20.1%

neutral or uncertain. The results of both Surveys showed that the majority of respondents did not support a change in the law on assisted dying. However, the number objecting to a change in legislation fell in 2014 by 10.7% from 73.2 to 65.5%, possibly indicating a shift in opinion. These results also show an increase of 2.5% in the number of members in favour of being actively involved in PAD, with a decrease of 1% in members opposed to taking part.

In addition to protecting patients, many doctors will also feel the need for protection. There are many factors that influence an individual's stance on PAD, religion being the most influential. Most envisaged a scenario where doctors will have the option to 'opt out' if the legislation were changed to protect doctors, who feel PAD is morally wrong. If 'opt out' were not adopted it could influence the type of person applying to medical school, and actually deter some individuals, irrevocably changing the landscape of the medical profession, especially if we again consider the power of culture and religion in these debates. Despite a number of bills and high-profile court cases in support of assisted dying, it continues to be an offence under UK law. In both 2006 and 2014, the majority of RCP members and fellows opposed a change in current legislation on assisted dying and favoured improvements in palliative care. Therefore, the RCP opposes any change in current legislation surrounding PAD, and maintains that good palliative and End-of-Life care is the mainstay in providing patients with a good and dignified death."

Dr David Holding

Sources: British Medical Association, "End of life care and physician assisted dying" (London, BMA, 2016). Future Healthcare Journal, (2018), Vol 5, No 1, 30-34: Authors: Karen Porter and Katherine G. Warburton.

Chapter Six:
Biomedical Ethics and Euthanasia

This final chapter examines the distinctions between killing and letting die, intending and foreseeing harmful outcomes, withholding and withdrawing life-sustaining treatments, and ordinary and extraordinary treatments.

Much debate concerning the forgoing of life-sustaining treatment has centred on the *omission-commission* distinction. In particular, the distinction between withholding (not starting) and withdrawing (stopping) treatment.

Many medical professionals and family members feel justified in withholding treatments that have never actually been started but not withdrawing treatments already in progress. Feelings of reluctance about withdrawing treatments are understandable, but the distinction between withdrawing and withholding treatments is contentious.

Both not starting and stopping can cause a patient's death, and both can be instances of 'allowing to die'. Also, both can even be instances of 'killing'.

Courts of law recognise that individuals can commit a crime by omission if they have an obligation to act. However, such a judgment depends on whether a physician has an obligation either not to withhold or not to withdraw treatment. If a physician has a duty to treat, then the omission of treatment breaches the duty, whether withholding or withdrawing is involved. However, if a physician does not have a duty to treat or not to treat, then the omission of either type involves no moral violation.

Put simply, if the physician has a duty not to treat, then it would be a moral violation not to withdraw a treatment that has already begun. Only after starting treatments will it be possible, in many cases, to make a proper diagnosis and prognosis and balance prospective benefits and burdens.

Both patients and relatives often feel less stressed and more in control if they can reverse or otherwise change a decision to treat once that treatment has started. Decisions about beginning or ending treatment should be based on considerations of the patient's rights and welfare as judged by a competent patient or relatives.

Conceptual Questions about the Nature of Ethical Killing and Letting Die

Can we define 'killing' and 'letting die' so that they are conceptually distinct and do not overlap?

In ordinary language, killing is casual action that brings about death, whereas letting die is the intentional avoidance of casual intervention so that disease, system failure or injury causes death.

However, conventional definitions are

unsatisfactory for drawing a sharp distinction between killing and letting die.

They allow many acts of letting die count as killing, thereby defeating any distinction. For example, under these definitions, health professionals kill patients when they intentionally let them die in circumstances in which a duty exists to keep the patients alive.

Killing and letting die do not occur by accident, chance or mishap and are not mutually exclusive concepts.

One person can kill another by intentionally allowing the other to die so that killing can occur by omission as well as by commission. However, the meanings of killing and letting die are vague and contestable.

'Letting die' is acceptable in medicine under one of two justifying conditions; a medical technology is futile, or patients/their representatives have validly refused a medical technology.

Killing, by contrast, is connected in medicine to unacceptable acts. In general, the term 'killing' does not necessarily entail a wrongful act or a crime.

The rule of 'Do Not Kill' is not absolute.

Hence, standard justifications for killing, such as in self-defence, prevent us from prejudging an action as wrong because it results in a killing. Correctly labelling an act as 'killing' or as 'letting die' does not determine that one form of action is better or wrong or more or less justified than the other.

Neither killing nor letting die are wrongful per se,

and in this regard, they are distinguished from murder, which is wrongful per se.

A judgment that an act of either killing or letting die is justified or unjustified entails that we know something about the act besides these characteristics.

We may require to know about the actor's motive (whether it is benevolent or malicious), the patient's or representative's 'request', or the act's consequences.

Is forgoing life-sustaining treatment killing or allowing to die?

Many writers in medicine, law and ethics have construed a physician's intentionally forgoing a medical technology as 'letting die' rather than 'killing', if and only if an underlying disease or injury causes death.

According to this doctrine, when physicians withhold or withdraw medical technology, a natural death occurs because natural conditions do what they would have done if the technology had not been initiated.

By contrast, killings occur when acts of persons rather than natural conditions cause death. However, though this view is influential in law and medicine, it is seriously flawed.

The forgoing of medical technology is validly authorised, and for that reason, it is justified. If the physician's forgoing of technology were unjustified and a person died from 'natural' causes of injury or disease, the result would be unjustified killing. The validity of the authorisation determines the morality of the action.

Physicians do not injure, maltreat or kill patients when they withhold or withdraw medical technology and thereby physically cause death. A physician is morally and legally obligated to recognise and act upon a valid refusal of treatment since a valid refusal of treatment binds the physician.

From a legal perspective, liability should not be imposed on physicians and relatives unless they have an obligation to provide or continue the treatment. If no obligation to treat exists, then questions of causation and liability do not arise.

Under what conditions is it permissible for patients and health professionals to arrange for assisted suicide or voluntary active euthanasia?

For clarification, in assisted suicide, the final agent is the one whose death is brought about. In voluntary active euthanasia, the final agent is another party who has been authorised to act by the one whose death is brought about.

Many people both inside and outside medicine now believe that active physician assistance for a narrow group of seriously ill and dying patients at their request can be morally justified. To justify an act is distinct from justifying a practice or a policy that permits or even legitimates the act's performance.

A rule of practice or a public policy that prohibits various forms of assistance in dying in medicine may be justified, even if it excludes some acts of causing a person's death that are morally justifiable.

For example, a law might not permit physicians to use a drug overdose to cause death for a patient who suffers unbearable pain, will probably die within weeks, and requests assisted death. However, this same act might be justified in an individual case.

The problem is that practice or policy allowing physicians to intervene to cause deaths or help cause deaths runs risks of abuse on balance and might cause more harm than benefit. The argument is not that serious abuses will occur immediately but that they will grow incrementally over time.

Society could start by severely restricting the number of patients who qualify for assistance in dying but might later revise and loosen their restrictions so that cases of unjustified killing begin to occur.

Unscrupulous persons would learn how to abuse the system. The slope of the trail toward 'unjustified' taking of life will be so 'slippery' and precipitous that we ought never to get on it.

Many dismiss these 'slippery slope' arguments because of a lack of empirical evidence to support these claims. However, we should take some arguments of this form very seriously. They force us to consider whether unacceptable harm is likely to result from attractive and apparently innocent first steps.

If society removes certain restraints against interventions that cause death, psychological and social forces would likely make it more difficult to maintain the relevant distinctions in medical practice. Voluntary active euthanasia invites social changes, leading to non-voluntary euthanasia (an act of killing a person who is incapable of making informed consent).

This 'slippery slope' argument becomes compelling

when we consider the effects of social discrimination based on disability. An increasing number of newborns with disabilities survive at a high cost to the public, and a growing number of ageing persons with medical problems require larger proportions of public financial resources.

If rules permitting voluntary active euthanasia become public policy, the risk increases that persons in these populations will be harmed. The risk increases further when families and health professionals abandon treatments for disabled newborns and severely brain-damaged adults.

Moreover, if decision-makers determine that some newborns and adults have overly burdensome conditions or lives with no value, the same logic can be extended elsewhere. Also affected could be other populations of feeble, debilitated and seriously ill patients who are financial and emotional burdens on families and society.

Many of these circumstances are relevantly similar to circumstances that already provide the leading justification for third-party decisions to withdraw or withhold life-support. Often the patients did not request these omissions and left no advance directive. For example, it takes little imagination to suppose that many parents would, if given the opportunity, withhold life-sustaining technologies from their newborns because of disabilities such as blindness, retardation and malformation.

Rules in our moral code against passively or actively causing the death of another person are not 'isolated fragments'. They are threads in a fabric of rules that support respect for human life.

The more threads we remove, the weaker the fabric may become. If we focus on modifying attitudes, not only on rules, then shifts in public policy may also erode the general attitude of respect for life.

Rules against bringing about another's death also provide a basis of trust between patients and health care professionals. We may risk a loss of public trust if physicians become agents of active euthanasia, in addition to healers and caregivers.

Likewise, we may also risk a loss of trust if patients and families believe that physicians are abandoning them in their suffering because they lack the courage and will to offer the assistance needed in the darkest hours of their lives.

The ultimate success or failure of 'slippery slope' arguments against assistance in dying depends on speculative predictions of a progressive erosion of moral restraints. If dire consequences flow from the legal legitimation of assisted suicide or voluntary active euthanasia, these arguments are cogent, and such practices are justifiably prohibited. However, how good is the evidence that dire consequences will occur?

Arguments on every side are speculative and analogical, and different assessors of the same evidence reach different conclusions. The frontier of the social and legal acceptance of expanded rights to control one's death has shifted from 'refusal' of treatment to 'request' for assistance in dying. Now that law and morality ensure that competent patients have a right to refuse treatment and health professionals have an obligation to implement the refusals may have turned their attention to whether patients have a similar right to request the assistance of physicians willing to help them die.

This strategy rests on the premise that professional ethics and law reform is needed. There is an apparent inconsistency between the strong rights of autonomy that allow persons in grave circumstances to refuse treatment to bring about their deaths and the apparent denial of a similar autonomy right to arrange for death by mutual agreement between patient and physician under equally grave circumstances.

The argument for reform seems particularly compelling when a condition has become overwhelmingly burdensome for a patient, pain management is inadequate, and only a physician can and is willing to bring relief. At present, medicine and law are in the awkward position of having to say to such patients:

"If you were on life-sustaining treatment, you would have a right to withdraw the treatment, and then we could let you die. But since you are not, we can only allow you to refuse nutrition and hydration or give you palliative care until you die of a 'natural' death, however painful, undignified and costly".

A health professional is obligated to honour an autonomous refusal of life-saving technology, but he or she is not obligated to honour an autonomous request for assistance in dying. A physician's specific responsibilities to a patient may depend on the nature of the request made and the nature of the preestablished patient-physician relationship.

If a person freely elects and authorises death and makes an independent judgment that the event constitutes a personal benefit rather than a setback to his or her interests, then active assistance in dying at the person's request involves no harm or moral wrong. Suppose letting die based on valid refusals does not harm or wrong persons who died earlier than they would have. How can assisted suicide or voluntary euthanasia harm or wrong persons who make autonomous choices to die earlier than they would otherwise?

In each case, persons seek what, for them, in their bleak circumstances, is the best means of quitting life. The person searching for assisted suicide, the person who seeks active euthanasia, and the person who foregoes life-sustaining technology to end life may be identically situated regarding prognosis and suffering. They simply select a different means to end their lives.

Assisting an autonomous person at his or her request to bring about death shows respect for the person's autonomous choices. Similarly, denying the person access to other willing and qualified individuals to comply with the request shows a fundamental disrespect for the person's autonomy.

From a purely social and legal perspective, there may be good grounds for more active protecting one type of patient than another.

The opponents of the Netherlands' approach to euthanasia have expressed concerns that the grounds for its exercise will inevitably become more trivial until what matters is not the grounds for wanting to die but the want itself. This could rapidly lead to an acceptance of euthanasia in the face of relatively minor discomfort or of conditions that, although distressing, are not necessarily permanent or terminal.

The pioneering legislation in the Netherlands has not led to many other jurisdictions following suit. However, it would not be surprising if this situation were to persist, given that acceptance of a practice in one jurisdiction often influences the decision to allow the practice elsewhere.

Selected Bibliography

Battin, M, 'Voluntary Euthanasia and the Rise of Abuse: Can We Learn Anything From the Netherlands?' (1992) 20, *Law, Medicine and Health Care*, 133.

Brazier, M, *Medicine, Patients and the Law*, 3rd Edition, (Penguin Books, London, 2003)

Brewin, TB, 'Voluntary Euthanasia', (1986), 1, *The Lancet*, 1085).

Byrne, P, (ed), *Medicine, Medical Ethics and the Value of Life*, (John Wiley, Chichester, 1990).

Campbell, AV, *Moral Dilemmas in Medicine*, (Edinburgh Churchill Livingstone, 1975).

Churchill, IR & King, NM, 'Physician-Assisted Suicide, Euthanasia or Withdrawal of Treatment', (1997) *BMJ*, 315, 137.

Dyer, C, 'GMC Tempers Justice with Mercy in Cox Case', (1992), *BMJ*, 305.

Dworkin, R, *Life's Dominion: An Argument about Abortion and Euthanasia* (London, Harper Collins, 1993).

Davies, M, *Textbook on Medical Law*, 2nd Edition, (Oxford University Press, 1998).

Fenwick, A J, 'Applying Best Interests to "Persistent

Vegetative State": A Principled Distortion?' *Journal of Medical Ethics*, 1998, 24.

Finnis, JM, 'Bland: Crossing the Rubicon?' (1993, *Law Quarterly Review,* 109, 329).

General Medical Council: *Withholding and Withdrawing Life-Prolonging Treatments: Good Practice in Decision Making,* (August, 2002). www. gmc-uk.org/standards/whwd.

Glover, J, *Causing Death and Saving Life,* (Penguin, Harmondsworth, 1988).

Gormally, L, *Euthanasia, Clinical Practice and the Law,* (London, Linacre Centre,1994).

Griffiths, J, 'Assisted Suicide in the Netherlands: The Chabot Case', (1995, *Medical Law Review,* 58, 232).

Harris, J, *The Value of Life: An Introduction to Medical Ethics,* (London, Routledge, 1985).

Harris, J (ed), *Bioethics,* (Oxford University Press, 2001).

Hellema, H, 'Euthanasia – 2% of Dutch Deaths', (1991) *BMJ*, 303, 877.

Hellema, H, 'Dutch Doctors Support Life Termination in Dementia' (1993) *BMJ*, 306, 1364.

Henden, H, 'Seduced by Death: Doctors, Patients and the Dutch Cure' (1995) *Law and Medicine,* 123.

House of Lords, *Report on the Select Committee on Medical Ethics,* HL Paper 21-2 (1994).

Humphrey, D & Wickett, A, *The Right to Die: Understanding Euthanasia,* (New York, Harper Rowe,

1986).

Kennedy, I, *Unmasking Medicine,* (London, Paladen,1983).

Kennedy, I & Grubb, A, *'Medical Law'* 3rd Edit. (Butterworths, London, 2000).

Kennedy, I, 'Switching Off Life Support Machines: The Legal Implications' (1977) *Criminal Law Review,* 443.

Keown, J (ed), *Euthanasia Examined,* (Cambridge University Press, 1995).

Keown, J, 'The Law and Practice of Euthanasia in the Netherlands' (1992) *Law Quarterly Review,* 108, 51.

Kuhse, H, *The Sanctity of Life Doctrine in Medicine: A Critique* (Oxford University Press, 1987).

Lenham, D, *'The Right to Choose to Die with Dignity',* (1990), *Criminal Law Review.*

Leenen, HJ, Euthanasia, assistance to suicide and the law: Developments in the Netherlands, (1987) *Health Policy.*

Mason, JK, Smith, RM & Laurie, GT, *Law and Medical Ethics,* 6th Edition, (Butterworths, London, 2002).

Rachells, J, *The End of Life: Euthanasia and Morality* (Oxford University Press,1987).

Royal Society of Medicine: *'On Dying and Dying Well: Legal Aspects'* (Transactions 70, 73, 1977).

Singer, P, *Practical Ethics* (Cambridge University Press, 1979).

Singer, P, *Rethinking Life and Death: The Collapse of our Traditional Ethics* (Oxford University Press, 1995).

Skegg, PD, *Law, Ethics and Medicine: Studies in Medical Law*, (Oxford, Clarendon Press, 1988).

Thompson, I, (ed), *Dilemmas of Dying: A Study in the Ethics of Terminal Care* (Edinburgh University Press, 1979).

Voluntary Euthanasia Society: *A Plea for Legislation to Permit Voluntary Euthanasia* (Voluntary Euthanasia Society, London, 1970).

Wise, J, *'Public Supports Euthanasia for Most Separate Cases'* (1996, BMJ, 313, 1423).

Printed in Great Britain
by Amazon